BUG HUNTING 101

NOVICE TO VIRTUOSO

WEB APPLICATION SECURITY FOR ETHICAL HACKERS

4 BOOKS IN 1

BOOK 1
BUG HUNTING: A NOVICE'S GUIDE TO SOFTWARE VULNERABILITIES

BOOK 2
INTERMEDIATE BUG HUNTING TECHNIQUES: FROM NOVICE TO SKILLED HUNTER

BOOK 3
ADVANCED BUG BOUNTY HUNTING: MASTERING THE ART OF CYBERSECURITY

BOOK 4
VIRTUOSO BUG HUNTER'S HANDBOOK: SECRETS OF THE ELITE ETHICAL HACKERS

ROB BOTWRIGHT

Published by Rob Botwright
Library of Congress Cataloging-in-Publication Data
ISBN 978-1-83938-573-5
Cover design by Rizzo

Disclaimer

The contents of this book are based on extensive research and the best available historical sources. However, the author and publisher make no claims, promises, or guarantees about the accuracy, completeness, or adequacy of the information contained herein. The information in this book is provided on an "as is" basis, and the author and publisher disclaim any and all liability for any errors, omissions, or inaccuracies in the information or for any actions taken in reliance on such information.

The opinions and views expressed in this book are those of the author and do not necessarily reflect the official policy or position of any organization or individual mentioned in this book. Any reference to specific people, places, or events is intended only to provide historical context and is not intended to defame or malign any group, individual, or entity.

The information in this book is intended for educational and entertainment purposes only. It is not intended to be a substitute for professional advice or judgment. Readers are encouraged to conduct their own research and to seek professional advice where appropriate.

Every effort has been made to obtain necessary permissions and acknowledgments for all images and other copyrighted material used in this book. Any errors or omissions in this regard are unintentional, and the author and publisher will correct them in future editions.

Introduction

Welcome to a transformative journey through the dynamic and ever-evolving world of cybersecurity and bug hunting. In this unique book bundle, "BUG HUNTING 101: NOVICE TO VIRTUOSO" and "WEB APPLICATION SECURITY FOR ETHICAL HACKERS," we embark on a comprehensive exploration of software vulnerabilities, ethical hacking, and the strategies employed by elite ethical hackers.

Cybersecurity has become an integral part of our modern digital landscape. With each passing day, the digital world expands, becoming more complex and interconnected. Alongside this growth, the potential for vulnerabilities and security threats also multiplies. It is within this landscape that ethical hackers and bug hunters emerge as the frontline defenders of digital security.

Our journey begins with "BOOK 1 - BUG HUNTING: A NOVICE'S GUIDE TO SOFTWARE VULNERABILITIES." Here, we cater to those taking their first steps into the captivating realm of bug hunting. We will guide you through the fundamental concepts of software vulnerabilities, ethical hacking, and the essential skills required to become a proficient bug hunter. With practical insights and real-world examples, this book lays the foundation for your bug hunting journey.

As we progress to "BOOK 2 - INTERMEDIATE BUG HUNTING TECHNIQUES: FROM NOVICE TO SKILLED HUNTER," we transition from novice to skilled hunters. This book equips you with intermediate bug hunting techniques, including in-depth vulnerability discovery, scanning, and enumeration. It's a pivotal stage in your journey, where you'll enhance your skills and gain confidence in tackling more complex security challenges.

In "BOOK 3 - ADVANCED BUG BOUNTY HUNTING: MASTERING THE ART OF CYBERSECURITY," we delve into the advanced realms of bug hunting and cybersecurity. Cryptographic flaws, network intrusion, and advanced exploitation techniques await your exploration. This book not only elevates your technical prowess but also guides you in strategically engaging with bug bounty programs.

Finally, "BOOK 4 - VIRTUOSO BUG HUNTER'S HANDBOOK: SECRETS OF THE ELITE ETHICAL HACKERS" opens the doors to the elite world of ethical hackers. Here, we reveal the mindset, techniques, and advanced artifacts employed by the virtuosos in the field. This book uncovers strategies for maximizing bug bounty program participation and addresses crucial legal and ethical considerations for those at the zenith of their bug hunting careers.

Together, these four books form a comprehensive roadmap for aspiring bug hunters and ethical hackers, taking you from novice to virtuoso. Throughout this journey, we will emphasize not only the acquisition of technical skills but also the ethical responsibility that comes with the power to identify and remediate vulnerabilities.

The digital world relies on individuals like you to ensure its security and integrity. As ethical hackers and bug hunters, your role is not just about finding and fixing vulnerabilities; it's about safeguarding the digital landscape for everyone.

So, join us as we embark on this enlightening journey through "BUG HUNTING 101: NOVICE TO VIRTUOSO" and "WEB APPLICATION SECURITY FOR ETHICAL HACKERS." Together, we will explore the depths of cybersecurity, uncover the secrets of bug hunting, and empower you to become a guardian of the digital realm.

BOOK 1
BUG HUNTING
A NOVICE'S GUIDE TO SOFTWARE VULNERABILITIES

ROB BOTWRIGHT

Chapter 1: Introduction to Bug Hunting

Bug hunting, also known as ethical hacking or security testing, holds a crucial role in today's digitally interconnected world. It involves the systematic search for security vulnerabilities within software, applications, networks, and systems, with the primary goal of identifying and mitigating these weaknesses before malicious actors can exploit them.

The significance of bug hunting extends far beyond the realm of cybersecurity experts and organizations; it impacts the daily lives of individuals who rely on technology for communication, business, and personal activities. In essence, bug hunting is about safeguarding the digital infrastructure that underpins our modern society.

At its core, bug hunting is driven by a profound sense of responsibility—a recognition that the digital landscape is fraught with potential threats, and that addressing these vulnerabilities is not only a professional duty but a moral obligation.

The consequences of failing to address these vulnerabilities can be severe. Malicious actors can exploit software weaknesses to steal sensitive data, disrupt critical infrastructure, compromise user privacy, and wreak havoc on a global scale.

Thus, bug hunting matters because it acts as a frontline defense against cyber threats, protecting not only businesses but also the individuals who entrust their personal information to digital systems. It contributes to the maintenance of trust in technology, which is essential for the functioning of modern society.

Furthermore, bug hunting plays a pivotal role in fostering innovation. By identifying and rectifying vulnerabilities early in the development process, it enables the creation of more secure and robust software and applications. This, in turn, leads to the development of cutting-edge technologies and services that drive economic growth and improve the quality of life.

The bug hunting community is a diverse and dynamic ecosystem, comprising cybersecurity professionals, ethical hackers, researchers, and enthusiasts. These individuals collaborate across borders and organizational boundaries, sharing knowledge and expertise to strengthen the collective defense against cyber threats.

As we embark on this journey into the world of bug hunting, it is important to acknowledge that it is not a solitary endeavor but a collaborative one. The collective effort of bug hunters worldwide is what makes it possible to identify and mitigate vulnerabilities effectively.

In the following chapters, we will explore various aspects of bug hunting, starting from the fundamentals and gradually delving into more advanced techniques and strategies. Whether you are a novice just beginning your bug hunting journey or an experienced hunter looking to refine your skills, there is something in these pages for everyone.

We will cover the different types of software vulnerabilities that bug hunters seek to uncover, including those that affect web applications, mobile apps, and networked systems.

Additionally, we will delve into the bug bounty programs and ethical hacking practices that provide bug hunters with the legal and ethical framework to operate within.

Setting up your bug hunting environment is a crucial step, as it ensures that you have the necessary tools and resources to conduct your bug hunting activities safely and effectively.

Information gathering and reconnaissance are fundamental aspects of bug hunting, helping you gather intelligence about your target and potential attack vectors.

Scanning and enumeration techniques are used to identify vulnerabilities and weaknesses in systems, allowing you to pinpoint areas of interest for further investigation.

Exploitation techniques form the heart of bug hunting, as they enable you to leverage vulnerabilities to gain unauthorized access or control over a system.

Reporting vulnerabilities effectively is not just about identifying issues but also communicating them to the relevant parties in a clear and concise manner.

Bug fixing and patch management are essential for organizations to address the vulnerabilities that bug hunters discover, ensuring the security and integrity of their systems.

Finally, continuous learning and advancing your skills are crucial in a field as dynamic as bug hunting, where new vulnerabilities and attack techniques emerge regularly.

Throughout this book, we will provide practical insights, real-world examples, and hands-on exercises to help you develop and hone your bug hunting skills.

Bug hunting is a discipline that demands a combination of technical prowess, creativity, and a deep understanding of software and systems. It is a journey that can be challenging and rewarding in equal measure.

As you progress through the chapters, you will gain the knowledge and confidence needed to embark on bug hunting missions, whether as an independent ethical hacker or as part of a bug bounty program.

Before we dive into the specifics, it is worth mentioning that bug hunting is not about breaking the law or engaging in malicious activities. Ethical bug hunters operate within a legal and moral framework, seeking authorization before probing systems for vulnerabilities and adhering to responsible disclosure practices.

In the digital age, the role of bug hunters has never been more critical. With the increasing complexity and interconnectivity of technology, the attack surface for potential vulnerabilities has expanded exponentially.

Cybersecurity threats are evolving rapidly, with attackers employing sophisticated techniques to breach systems and exploit weaknesses. Organizations and individuals alike are at risk, making it imperative to have skilled bug hunters who can identify and mitigate vulnerabilities proactively.

In the pages that follow, we will equip you with the knowledge, tools, and mindset needed to become a proficient bug hunter.

Whether you are an aspiring ethical hacker, a cybersecurity professional, or someone curious about the world of bug hunting, this book will serve as a valuable resource on your journey to mastering the art of cybersecurity through responsible and ethical bug hunting.

In the next chapter, we will explore the different types of software vulnerabilities that bug hunters commonly encounter, providing you with a foundational understanding of the vulnerabilities you will be seeking to uncover in your bug hunting endeavors.

The world of bug hunting is a vast and interconnected ecosystem, driven by a passionate and diverse community of individuals who are dedicated to making the digital world safer. This community spans across the globe, uniting people from different backgrounds, cultures, and expertise levels, all bound by a common goal: to identify and mitigate vulnerabilities in software and systems.

At the heart of the bug hunting community are cybersecurity professionals, ethical hackers, and security researchers who actively engage in finding and reporting vulnerabilities to the organizations and developers responsible for the affected software. They are the frontline defenders of the digital realm, tirelessly searching for weaknesses that could be exploited by malicious actors.

Bug hunters come from a wide range of backgrounds, from software engineers and IT professionals to hobbyists and students. What unites them is a shared enthusiasm for uncovering vulnerabilities and a commitment to ethical hacking practices. Many bug hunters are self-taught, learning through hands-on experience and continuous learning from the broader community.

Collaboration is a cornerstone of the bug hunting community. Bug hunters often share their findings, insights, and knowledge through various platforms, such as bug bounty forums, online communities, and social media. This collaborative spirit extends to the responsible disclosure of vulnerabilities, where hunters work with organizations to address and fix issues before they can be exploited by cybercriminals.

Bug bounty programs, offered by organizations to incentivize bug hunters to find and report vulnerabilities in their software, have played a significant role in nurturing and expanding the bug hunting community. These programs offer monetary rewards, recognition, and sometimes even employment opportunities to skilled hunters who uncover security flaws.

In addition to financial incentives, bug bounty programs provide bug hunters with a structured and ethical framework for their activities. This helps ensure that the discoveries made by hunters are used for the benefit of cybersecurity rather than malicious purposes.

Beyond bug bounties, the bug hunting community actively participates in Capture The Flag (CTF) competitions, hackathons, and security conferences. These events allow bug hunters to test their skills, learn from peers, and network with like-minded individuals who share their passion for cybersecurity.

The bug hunting community is not limited to technical experts alone. It also includes legal and compliance professionals who specialize in cybersecurity law and regulations. Their expertise is invaluable in navigating the legal and ethical aspects of bug hunting, ensuring that hunters operate within the bounds of the law.

Mentorship is a common practice within the bug hunting community, where experienced hunters guide and mentor newcomers, sharing their knowledge and providing support. This mentorship helps newcomers learn the ropes, avoid common pitfalls, and accelerate their growth as bug hunters.

Ethics and responsible disclosure are core principles upheld by the bug hunting community. Hunters understand the importance of notifying organizations about vulnerabilities promptly and allowing them time to fix the issues before making them public. This responsible approach ensures that security flaws are addressed without putting users or organizations at risk.

The bug hunting community also engages in continuous learning and skill development. With the ever-evolving landscape of cybersecurity, staying up-to-date with the latest attack techniques and defense strategies is essential. Bug hunters actively participate in online courses, workshops, and certifications to enhance their knowledge and skills.

Participation in the bug hunting community is not only about personal growth and professional development but also about making a positive impact on the digital world. Every vulnerability discovered and responsibly disclosed contributes to a more secure online environment for individuals, businesses, and organizations worldwide.

In essence, the bug hunting community embodies the spirit of collaboration, responsibility, and continuous improvement. It is a dynamic and inclusive community that welcomes individuals of all backgrounds who share a common passion for cybersecurity and the protection of the digital realm.

As you journey through the world of bug hunting, you will find yourself becoming a part of this vibrant and supportive community. Whether you are a novice taking your first steps or an experienced hunter looking to refine your skills, the bug hunting community is here to guide and inspire you on your path to becoming a proficient bug hunter.

In the next chapter, we will delve deeper into the various types of software vulnerabilities that bug hunters commonly encounter during their quests. Understanding these vulnerabilities is essential for any bug hunter, as it forms the foundation of their work in identifying and mitigating security weaknesses.

Chapter 2: Types of Software Vulnerabilities

Software vulnerabilities are like hidden traps within the digital landscape, waiting to be discovered and remedied by bug hunters and security experts. These vulnerabilities are weaknesses or flaws in software code that can be exploited by malicious actors to compromise the security, integrity, or availability of a system or application. They are often unintentional, the result of human error during the software development process.

One of the most common software vulnerabilities is the "Buffer Overflow." This vulnerability occurs when a program writes more data to a buffer or memory location than it can hold, potentially allowing an attacker to overwrite adjacent memory areas, execute arbitrary code, and gain unauthorized access.

Another prevalent vulnerability is "SQL Injection." In this scenario, an attacker injects malicious SQL code into user input fields, exploiting inadequate input validation. This can lead to unauthorized access to a database, data leakage, and even data manipulation.

"Cross-Site Scripting (XSS)" is a vulnerability that enables attackers to inject malicious scripts into web pages viewed by other users. This can lead to the theft of user data, session hijacking, and the spreading of malware.

Insecure authentication mechanisms are a common vulnerability, such as the "Weak Password Policies." These vulnerabilities can allow attackers to guess or crack passwords easily, gaining unauthorized access to user accounts or systems.

Security misconfigurations are prevalent as well. These occur when systems or applications are not properly configured or secured. For example, leaving default passwords in place or allowing unnecessary services to run can expose vulnerabilities.

The "Broken Authentication" vulnerability is another common issue, where flaws in the authentication process allow attackers to bypass login mechanisms or impersonate other users.

Insecure direct object references occur when an application provides access to objects (e.g., files, database records) based on user-supplied input. If not properly validated, attackers can manipulate input to gain unauthorized access to sensitive data.

"Sensitive Data Exposure" vulnerabilities can lead to the exposure of confidential information, such as passwords or credit card numbers. This often happens when data is not adequately encrypted or protected.

Inadequate security logging and monitoring can also be a vulnerability. Without proper monitoring, it becomes challenging to detect and respond to security incidents promptly.

Finally, "Security Through Obscurity" is a common misconception. Relying on secrecy for security rather than robust security practices can leave systems vulnerable when attackers discover hidden weaknesses.

Understanding these common software vulnerabilities is the first step towards effective bug hunting. It allows bug hunters to recognize the weak points in software and systems, helping them identify and report vulnerabilities responsibly.

In the following chapters, we will explore techniques and methodologies for detecting and mitigating these vulnerabilities, equipping you with the knowledge and skills needed to become a proficient bug hunter. Remember, bug hunting is not just about finding flaws but also about contributing to a safer digital world.

As you embark on your bug hunting journey, keep in mind that every vulnerability you uncover and report is a step toward enhancing cybersecurity. Your efforts, alongside those of the broader bug hunting community, play a vital role in safeguarding the digital realm for individuals and organizations alike.

In the next chapter, we will delve into bug bounty programs and ethical hacking practices, providing you with insights into the structured frameworks that enable bug hunters to operate responsibly and ethically. Understanding these frameworks is essential as you navigate the bug hunting landscape.

In the world of software vulnerabilities, there are common weaknesses that are well-known and frequently targeted by attackers, but there also exist rare and obscure vulnerabilities that are less understood and more challenging to detect. These uncommon vulnerabilities are like hidden gems waiting to be discovered by vigilant bug hunters who possess the curiosity and expertise to uncover the unexpected.

One category of rare vulnerabilities includes "Race Conditions." These occur when multiple processes or threads access shared resources simultaneously, leading to unpredictable behavior that can be exploited by attackers. Detecting and reproducing race conditions can be intricate tasks, requiring a deep understanding of the software's inner workings.

Another less common vulnerability is "Insecure Deserialization." This occurs when an application accepts serialized data without proper validation, potentially allowing attackers to execute arbitrary code during deserialization. Insecure deserialization vulnerabilities are not as frequently encountered as other types but can be extremely impactful when found.

Some vulnerabilities are rooted in complex cryptographic flaws. For instance, "Cryptographic Timing Attacks" rely on precise timing measurements to exploit weaknesses in cryptographic implementations. These vulnerabilities demand a high level of expertise in cryptography and precise timing measurements to detect and mitigate effectively.

"Side-Channel Attacks" are another category of rare vulnerabilities, where attackers gather information from the physical implementation of a cryptographic algorithm rather than breaking the algorithm itself. These attacks can involve monitoring power consumption, electromagnetic emissions, or other physical phenomena to extract cryptographic keys.

Rare vulnerabilities can also stem from unique architectural or design flaws. "Privilege Escalation through Hardware Features" is one such example. It involves exploiting hardware features or components to elevate privileges and gain unauthorized access to a system. These vulnerabilities require a deep understanding of both hardware and software interactions.

Moreover, "Firmware Vulnerabilities" are relatively less common but can have significant consequences. Firmware is the software embedded in hardware devices, and vulnerabilities in firmware can lead to device compromise or unauthorized control. Detecting and patching firmware vulnerabilities often require specialized tools and expertise.

In the realm of web security, "Client-Side Template Injection" vulnerabilities are less prevalent but can lead to severe consequences. Attackers exploit weaknesses in client-side template engines to execute malicious code on the client-side, potentially compromising user data or sessions.

Furthermore, "Supply Chain Attacks" are rare but impactful vulnerabilities that target the software supply chain. Attackers compromise software dependencies or repositories, inserting malicious code that can be unwittingly integrated into applications by developers. Detecting and mitigating supply chain attacks require heightened vigilance in software development practices.

"Zero-Click Vulnerabilities" are exceptionally elusive and rare. They enable attackers to compromise a system without any interaction or input from the user. These vulnerabilities often target applications that handle multimedia content, making them difficult to detect and mitigate.

It's important to recognize that rare and obscure vulnerabilities often require a unique set of skills and expertise to uncover and address. They may also demand a deep dive into specific domains such as cryptography, hardware, or low-level system interactions.

Bug hunters who specialize in uncovering these types of vulnerabilities are often regarded as experts in their respective fields. Their contributions to cybersecurity are invaluable, as they help protect against threats that may go unnoticed by less experienced hunters.

In your journey as a bug hunter, you may encounter both common and rare vulnerabilities. It's essential to approach each discovery with diligence and a commitment to responsible disclosure. By doing so, you contribute to the ongoing effort to strengthen digital security and protect users and organizations from the full spectrum of potential threats.

In the chapters that follow, we will continue to explore various aspects of bug hunting, including advanced techniques, methodologies, and strategies for identifying and mitigating vulnerabilities. Whether you are just starting or looking to advance your bug hunting skills, these insights will be valuable on your bug hunting journey.

Chapter 3: Bug Bounty Programs and Ethical Hacking

The world of ethical hacking is a dynamic and ever-evolving field that plays a pivotal role in defending against cyber threats and securing digital systems. Ethical hackers, often referred to as "white hat" hackers, are individuals or professionals who use their skills and knowledge to identify vulnerabilities in software, networks, and systems with the explicit goal of improving security.

Ethical hacking is built on a foundation of knowledge and expertise in cybersecurity principles, computer systems, and programming languages. Ethical hackers possess a deep understanding of how attackers think and operate, enabling them to anticipate and counteract potential threats effectively.

One of the fundamental principles of ethical hacking is the concept of "attack and defense." Ethical hackers leverage the same techniques and tools employed by malicious hackers to uncover vulnerabilities and weaknesses in systems. By doing so, they help organizations strengthen their defenses and mitigate potential risks.

Ethical hacking is guided by a strict code of ethics and legal boundaries. Unlike malicious hackers, ethical hackers operate within the confines of the law and adhere to responsible disclosure practices. They seek authorization before probing systems for vulnerabilities and report their findings to the relevant parties to facilitate remediation.

The primary goal of ethical hacking is to identify vulnerabilities before malicious hackers can exploit them. By proactively seeking and addressing weaknesses, organizations can reduce the likelihood of security breaches, data breaches, and other cyberattacks. Ethical hackers act as a first line of defense, helping organizations safeguard their digital assets.

Ethical hackers often engage in penetration testing, a structured approach to evaluating the security of systems and networks. Penetration testing involves simulating real-world attack scenarios to assess the effectiveness of security measures and identify potential weaknesses.

Bug bounty programs are a common practice in the world of ethical hacking. These programs are offered by organizations as a way to incentivize ethical hackers to discover and report vulnerabilities in their software or systems. Ethical hackers who participate in bug bounty programs may receive monetary rewards, recognition, or other incentives for their findings.

Ethical hackers work closely with organizations to ensure that vulnerabilities are remediated promptly and effectively. They collaborate with security teams and developers to provide guidance on mitigating risks and implementing security best practices.

In addition to vulnerability discovery, ethical hackers often play a vital role in incident response and threat analysis. Their expertise in understanding attack techniques and vulnerabilities allows them to assist organizations in identifying and mitigating security incidents.

Continuous learning and skill development are essential in the world of ethical hacking. Cyber threats are constantly evolving, and ethical hackers must stay updated on the latest attack techniques, vulnerabilities, and security trends. This requires a commitment to ongoing education and certification in cybersecurity.

Ethical hackers often pursue certifications such as Certified Ethical Hacker (CEH), Certified Information Systems Security Professional (CISSP), or Offensive Security Certified

Professional (OSCP) to validate their expertise and demonstrate their commitment to ethical hacking practices.

The role of an ethical hacker is not limited to uncovering vulnerabilities; it also involves educating and raising awareness about cybersecurity. Ethical hackers often conduct security training sessions and workshops for organizations, helping employees and stakeholders understand the importance of security hygiene and best practices.

Ethical hacking is a rewarding and fulfilling career path for individuals who are passionate about cybersecurity and enjoy solving complex puzzles. It offers the opportunity to make a significant impact on the security of digital systems and contribute to the protection of sensitive data and critical infrastructure.

As you delve deeper into the world of ethical hacking, you will explore advanced techniques, methodologies, and strategies for uncovering vulnerabilities and improving security. Your journey as an ethical hacker will be characterized by continuous learning, collaboration, and a commitment to ethical and responsible hacking practices.

In the chapters ahead, we will delve into various aspects of ethical hacking, including the tools of the trade, penetration testing methodologies, and practical exercises to hone your skills. Whether you are a novice or an experienced professional, the world of ethical hacking offers endless opportunities for growth and contribution to the cybersecurity landscape.

Navigating bug bounty platforms is a crucial skill for any aspiring ethical hacker or bug hunter. These platforms serve as the bridge between ethical hackers and organizations seeking to identify and remediate vulnerabilities in their software and systems. They provide a structured and secure environment for hunters to participate in bug bounty programs, uncover vulnerabilities, and receive rewards for their findings.

Bug bounty platforms act as intermediaries, connecting ethical hackers with organizations looking to improve their cybersecurity. These platforms host a variety of bug bounty programs offered by organizations of all sizes, ranging from startups to large enterprises and even government agencies.

The first step in navigating bug bounty platforms is to choose the right platform for your bug hunting journey. There are several bug bounty platforms available, each with its own unique features and program offerings. It's essential to research and select a platform that aligns with your interests and expertise.

Once you've chosen a bug bounty platform, the next step is to create an account. You'll need to provide the necessary information, including your name, contact details, and payment preferences, as many platforms offer monetary rewards for successful bug reports. It's crucial to provide accurate and up-to-date information to ensure smooth interactions with the platform and organizations.

After creating your account, you can start exploring the bug bounty programs available on the platform. Bug bounty programs are typically categorized based on the type of software or system they cover, such as web applications, mobile apps, network infrastructure, or IoT devices. You can browse through the programs and choose those that match your skills and interests.

Program details are essential to review before you start hunting for bugs. Each program will have specific rules, guidelines, and scope documents that outline what is and isn't in scope for testing. Understanding the scope is crucial to ensure that your bug reports are eligible for rewards. It's also important to familiarize yourself with the rules and disclosure policies of the platform to ensure responsible and ethical bug hunting.

Once you've identified a bug bounty program that interests you and falls within your expertise, you can start testing the target systems or applications. This involves identifying vulnerabilities, exploiting them to demonstrate their impact, and documenting your findings thoroughly. It's essential to follow the rules and guidelines provided by the program to ensure your submissions are valid.

When you discover a potential vulnerability, you can report it through the bug bounty platform's reporting mechanism. This typically involves providing a detailed description of the vulnerability, including steps to reproduce it, its potential impact, and any supporting evidence you may have. Clear and concise reporting is essential to help organizations understand and address the issue effectively.

Communication with the organization is a crucial aspect of bug hunting through bug bounty platforms. You may need to interact with the organization's security or development teams to provide additional information, clarify details, or verify that the vulnerability has been fixed. Effective communication ensures that both parties work together to resolve the issue.

Bug bounty platforms often have a triage process in place to evaluate bug reports. During triage, the platform or organization assesses the validity and severity of the reported vulnerability. They may also assign a bounty amount based on the severity and impact of the bug. This process helps ensure fair compensation for ethical hackers.

Once a vulnerability is validated and fixed, organizations typically reward ethical hackers with monetary payouts, often referred to as bounties. The amount of the bounty can vary widely depending on the severity of the vulnerability, the organization's policies, and the platform's guidelines.

Some bug hunters earn substantial rewards for their findings.

It's important to note that not all bug reports will result in bounties. Some reports may be considered out of scope, duplicates of existing reports, or not severe enough to warrant a reward. However, ethical hackers still contribute to the improvement of security by identifying and reporting these vulnerabilities.

Building a reputation as a skilled bug hunter on bug bounty platforms can lead to more opportunities and higher payouts. Organizations often recognize and appreciate the expertise of experienced hunters and may invite them to participate in private bug bounty programs or even offer them employment or consultancy opportunities.

Navigating bug bounty platforms requires a combination of technical skills, ethical behavior, and effective communication. It's a journey that offers both personal and professional growth while contributing to the overall security of the digital landscape. As you explore bug bounty platforms and participate in programs, you'll gain valuable experience and knowledge in the field of ethical hacking.

In the chapters ahead, we will delve deeper into bug hunting techniques, strategies, and advanced methodologies to help you become a proficient bug hunter. Whether you're a beginner or an experienced hacker, bug bounty platforms provide a platform for continuous learning and skill development in the world of ethical hacking.

Chapter 4: Setting Up Your Bug Hunting Environment

Selecting the right tools is a pivotal aspect of bug hunting, as they empower you to efficiently identify vulnerabilities and conduct thorough assessments of software and systems. These tools, both open-source and commercial, are instrumental in your bug hunting arsenal. Your choice of tools should align with your expertise, the specific bug bounty program, and the target systems or applications you are testing.

One of the fundamental categories of tools used in bug hunting is vulnerability scanners. These automated tools are designed to identify known vulnerabilities in web applications, networks, and systems by scanning for common security issues. Examples of vulnerability scanners include Nessus, OpenVAS, and Burp Suite.

Web application scanners are a subset of vulnerability scanners tailored to identifying security weaknesses in web applications. They simulate attacks on web applications, detect vulnerabilities such as SQL injection and cross-site scripting (XSS), and provide detailed reports for remediation. Tools like OWASP ZAP and Acunetix fall into this category.

Network scanners are invaluable for assessing network security. They scan network infrastructure, identify open ports, services, and potential vulnerabilities, helping you understand the network's attack surface. Nmap and Wireshark are widely used network scanning tools.

While automated scanners are efficient for certain tasks, manual testing tools are equally important in bug hunting. Manual testing tools allow ethical hackers to conduct in-depth assessments, identify complex vulnerabilities, and simulate real-world attack scenarios.

Web proxies like Burp Suite and OWASP ZAP enable manual testing of web applications. They intercept and analyze HTTP requests and responses, making it possible to discover issues such as parameter manipulation, session fixation, and authentication flaws.

Exploitation frameworks, such as Metasploit, provide a range of pre-built exploits and payloads for testing vulnerabilities. These frameworks enable ethical hackers to simulate attacks and assess the severity of identified vulnerabilities.

Code analysis tools, like static and dynamic application security testing (SAST and DAST) tools, are essential for finding vulnerabilities in the source code of web applications. SAST tools, such as Checkmarx and Fortify, analyze source code for potential issues. DAST tools, like OWASP OWTF and AppSpider, test web applications by simulating attacks.

Packet sniffers and network analysis tools, including Wireshark and Tcpdump, help you inspect network traffic in real-time. These tools are valuable for identifying network-level vulnerabilities and monitoring traffic for suspicious activities.

Reverse engineering tools, such as IDA Pro and Ghidra, are crucial for analyzing binaries, firmware, and software applications. Reverse engineering allows ethical hackers to uncover vulnerabilities hidden within compiled code.

Forensic tools, like Autopsy and EnCase, are used for digital forensics and incident response. They help investigate security incidents, analyze compromised systems, and gather evidence for further analysis.

Open-source intelligence (OSINT) tools, such as Maltego and Shodan, enable ethical hackers to gather information about their targets. OSINT tools help identify potential attack vectors and vulnerabilities in target organizations.

Payload generators and scripting languages, like Python and Ruby, are essential for creating custom payloads and exploits. These tools provide flexibility in crafting tailored attacks and assessing the impact of vulnerabilities.

Choosing the right tools for bug hunting requires careful consideration of your objectives and the specific bug bounty program or project you are working on. Your selection should align with the type of software or system you are testing and your expertise level.

It's also important to stay updated with the latest tools and technologies in the cybersecurity field. The bug hunting landscape is constantly evolving, with new tools and techniques emerging regularly. Engaging with the bug hunting community, attending conferences, and participating in training programs can help you discover and learn about innovative tools and practices.

Furthermore, the ethical and responsible use of tools is a core principle of bug hunting. Always ensure that you have proper authorization to conduct assessments, respect the scope and rules of bug bounty programs, and adhere to ethical hacking guidelines. Misuse of tools or unauthorized testing can lead to legal and ethical consequences.

In summary, choosing the right tools is a critical aspect of bug hunting that empowers you to efficiently identify vulnerabilities and assess software and systems. By selecting tools that align with your expertise and objectives, you can enhance your bug hunting capabilities and contribute to the security of digital environments.

Creating a secure testing environment is a foundational step in bug hunting, as it provides a safe and controlled space to assess and exploit vulnerabilities without risking harm to production systems or sensitive data. This controlled environment is commonly referred to as a "lab" or "sandbox," and its importance cannot be overstated. Your ability to simulate real-world attack scenarios and test potential vulnerabilities hinges on the security and stability of this testing environment.

The first consideration when establishing a secure testing environment is isolation. It's crucial to isolate the lab environment from the production network to prevent any accidental or malicious impact on live systems. This isolation can be achieved by using physical or virtual separation, such as network segmentation or virtual local area networks (VLANs).

Another key aspect of isolation is the use of dedicated hardware or virtual machines (VMs) for testing. By setting up separate systems for bug hunting activities, you minimize the risk of unintended consequences, such as accidentally disrupting critical services or exposing sensitive information.

The operating system (OS) and software used in your testing environment should be carefully selected and configured. It's essential to use OS and software versions that mirror the target systems you plan to assess. This alignment ensures that your testing accurately reflects real-world scenarios and vulnerabilities.

To enhance security, you should harden the lab systems by disabling unnecessary services, applying security patches, and configuring firewall rules to restrict network access. Additionally, you can implement host-based intrusion detection systems (HIDS) to monitor system activity and detect potential security threats.

The lab should also include the tools and software necessary for your bug hunting activities. This includes vulnerability scanners, penetration testing frameworks, and other security assessment tools. Keeping your toolkit up-to-date is essential to leverage the latest features and bug fixes.

Security controls like antivirus software and intrusion prevention systems (IPS) should be disabled or configured not to interfere with your testing activities. These controls may block or alert on your activities, leading to inaccurate results.

Network monitoring and logging are critical components of a secure testing environment. By monitoring network traffic and maintaining detailed logs, you can track your activities, identify potential issues, and analyze the impact of vulnerabilities you uncover. Proper logging also aids in incident response and forensic analysis.

Access controls within the lab should be well-defined and strictly enforced. Only authorized personnel should have access to the testing environment, and strong authentication mechanisms should be in place. Role-based access control (RBAC) can help manage and restrict access based on individual responsibilities.

Data management is an important consideration when setting up a lab environment. Ensure that any data used for testing, such as databases, files, or user accounts, is properly sanitized and anonymized to prevent accidental exposure of sensitive information.

Backup and recovery procedures should be established to mitigate the risk of data loss or system failures during testing. Regularly backing up lab configurations, data, and snapshots of virtual machines can help ensure continuity in your bug hunting activities.

It's also advisable to have a rollback plan in place to quickly revert changes or configurations that may have unintended consequences. This plan allows you to maintain the stability of the lab environment and recover from any issues that may arise.

Lastly, keep in mind that maintaining a secure testing environment is an ongoing process. Regularly update and patch the lab systems, review access controls, and test the environment's resilience to attacks and vulnerabilities. Staying vigilant and proactive in maintaining security ensures that your testing environment remains a reliable and safe space for bug hunting activities.

In summary, creating a secure testing environment is a fundamental step in bug hunting, enabling you to assess vulnerabilities and conduct tests without risking harm to production systems or data. Isolation, proper configuration, access controls, and ongoing maintenance are key factors in establishing and maintaining the security of your testing environment. By following these best practices, you can conduct effective and responsible bug hunting activities while minimizing potential risks.

Chapter 5: Information Gathering and Reconnaissance

Passive information gathering is a critical phase in bug hunting, serving as the foundation for understanding the target system or organization you plan to assess. In this phase, you adopt a role similar to that of an online detective, collecting valuable data and insights without directly interacting with the target. The information you gather during passive reconnaissance sets the stage for more focused and effective bug hunting activities.

One of the primary objectives of passive information gathering is to identify the digital footprint of the target. This digital footprint encompasses all the online assets, resources, and information associated with the target, such as websites, subdomains, IP addresses, and email addresses.

To begin the passive information gathering process, you can leverage various online tools and resources. Search engines, such as Google, Bing, and DuckDuckGo, are valuable starting points. By conducting advanced searches and using specific operators, you can narrow down search results to reveal relevant information about the target.

Web archives, like the Wayback Machine, provide historical snapshots of websites, allowing you to view past versions of web pages and track changes over time. This historical data can reveal valuable insights, such as deprecated features, previous vulnerabilities, or changes in website structure.

Publicly available databases and repositories can be valuable sources of information during passive reconnaissance. For domain-related data, you can use domain registration databases like WHOIS to discover details about domain ownership, registration dates, and contact information.

For identifying subdomains and associated services, tools like DNS reconnaissance and subdomain enumeration scripts can be employed. These tools probe DNS records to uncover subdomains and their corresponding IP addresses, giving you a comprehensive view of the target's online presence.

Reverse IP lookup services can provide insights into shared hosting environments and reveal other websites hosted on the same server or IP address. This information can be useful for identifying potential attack vectors or targets.

Email addresses associated with the target can also be valuable during passive reconnaissance. Tools like theHarvester and EmailHunter can search the web for email addresses associated with the target organization, helping you establish contact points for further research or communication.

Publicly available documents and files can offer valuable insights as well. You can search for PDFs, documents, and spreadsheets related to the target, which may contain sensitive information or clues about the organization's infrastructure and operations.

Social media platforms are rich sources of information, providing details about employees, partnerships, events, and even potential vulnerabilities. You can investigate the target's social media profiles and monitor conversations or mentions related to the organization.

Online forums and communities frequented by employees or users of the target system can be treasure troves of information. By participating in discussions or monitoring forum threads, you can gain insights into common issues, technologies in use, and potential vulnerabilities.

Using passive information gathering techniques, ethical hackers can create a comprehensive profile of the target organization's online presence, infrastructure, and potential attack surfaces. This information serves as a roadmap for subsequent bug hunting activities, helping you identify potential vulnerabilities and attack vectors.

It's important to note that passive information gathering should always adhere to legal and ethical guidelines. You should respect the target's privacy and terms of service, avoiding any intrusive or harmful activities. Furthermore, ensure that you have proper authorization to conduct passive reconnaissance, especially in the context of bug bounty programs or ethical hacking engagements.

As you gather information passively, it's essential to maintain meticulous records of your findings. Documenting the data you collect, the sources you used, and any insights you uncover is crucial for effective bug hunting. Organizing your findings in a structured manner helps you maintain clarity and focus throughout the bug hunting process.

In summary, passive information gathering is a foundational phase in bug hunting, enabling ethical hackers to understand their target's digital footprint and identify potential vulnerabilities. By leveraging various online tools and resources, ethical hackers can collect valuable data and insights while adhering to legal and ethical principles. This phase sets the stage for more targeted and effective bug hunting activities, increasing the likelihood of uncovering critical vulnerabilities and contributing to improved cybersecurity.

Active reconnaissance techniques are a crucial component of bug hunting, providing a deeper level of insight into the target system or organization by actively probing and interacting with it. Unlike passive reconnaissance, which focuses on collecting publicly available information, active reconnaissance involves direct engagement and interaction with the target to identify vulnerabilities, misconfigurations, and potential attack vectors.

One of the primary goals of active reconnaissance is to gather information about the target's infrastructure, network topology, and exposed services. This information helps ethical hackers understand the attack surface and identify potential entry points for further assessment.

Port scanning is a fundamental active reconnaissance technique used to identify open ports on a target system. By sending specially crafted packets to the target, ethical hackers can determine which ports are listening and potentially running services. Tools like Nmap and Masscan are commonly used for port scanning.

Service enumeration follows port scanning and involves identifying the specific services running on open ports. This step is essential for understanding the potential vulnerabilities associated with each service. Ethical hackers can use banner grabbing techniques to extract version information and service details.

Vulnerability scanning is a critical aspect of active reconnaissance, as it involves the automated identification of known vulnerabilities in services or applications running on the target system. Vulnerability scanners like Nessus and OpenVAS compare the target's software versions with a database of known vulnerabilities to generate reports.

In addition to identifying vulnerabilities, ethical hackers may perform fingerprinting to gather information about the target's operating system, web server, or application framework. Fingerprinting techniques involve sending specific requests or probes and analyzing the responses to determine the target's characteristics.

Active reconnaissance also encompasses directory and file enumeration for web applications. Tools like Dirb and Gobuster are used to discover hidden directories, files, and resources that may not be directly linked from the website's main pages. This process can reveal potential attack vectors and sensitive information.

Web application testing is a critical component of active reconnaissance for web-based targets. Ethical hackers use techniques such as web crawling and manual exploration to identify potential security issues, including SQL injection, cross-site scripting (XSS), and other vulnerabilities. Web vulnerability scanners like Burp Suite and OWASP ZAP automate some of these tasks.

Brute-force attacks are employed in active reconnaissance to identify weak or easily guessable credentials for authentication. Tools like Hydra and Medusa can attempt various combinations of usernames and passwords to gain unauthorized access to services or applications.

While active reconnaissance techniques provide valuable insights, it's essential to conduct them responsibly and with proper authorization. Unauthorized or aggressive scanning can disrupt target systems, violate terms of service, and potentially lead to legal consequences.

Always ensure that you have explicit permission to perform active reconnaissance on the target.

Furthermore, it's crucial to be mindful of the impact of active reconnaissance on the target's resources and performance. Excessive scanning or probing can trigger intrusion detection systems (IDS) or raise alarms, leading to unwanted attention or countermeasures.

Active reconnaissance techniques require a systematic and structured approach to ensure thorough coverage of the target environment. Ethical hackers often create reconnaissance plans that outline the specific techniques, tools, and goals for each phase of active reconnaissance.

As you conduct active reconnaissance, maintain detailed records of your findings and activities. Documenting the results of port scans, service enumeration, vulnerability assessments, and other actions is essential for a comprehensive understanding of the target and the subsequent phases of bug hunting.

In summary, active reconnaissance techniques play a vital role in bug hunting by actively probing and interacting with the target to identify vulnerabilities and attack vectors. These techniques encompass port scanning, service enumeration, vulnerability scanning, fingerprinting, directory and file enumeration, web application testing, brute-force attacks, and more. Ethical hackers must conduct active reconnaissance responsibly, with proper authorization and a focus on minimizing disruption to the target. By employing these techniques effectively, bug hunters can uncover vulnerabilities and contribute to improved cybersecurity.

Chapter 6: Scanning and Enumeration

Network scanning methods are essential tools in the arsenal of ethical hackers, enabling them to uncover vulnerabilities, assess network security, and identify potential attack vectors. These methods involve systematically probing and examining a network to gain insights into its structure, services, and potential weaknesses.

One of the primary objectives of network scanning is to discover open ports and services running on target systems. Port scanning techniques, such as SYN scanning, connect scanning, and UDP scanning, allow ethical hackers to identify listening ports and the associated services. This information forms the foundation for further assessments.

In addition to port scanning, banner grabbing is a valuable technique used during network scanning. Banner grabbing involves connecting to open ports and retrieving service banners or headers, which often contain information about the software version and service details. Ethical hackers use this information to assess potential vulnerabilities associated with specific services.

Operating system fingerprinting is another aspect of network scanning that helps identify the underlying operating system of a target system. Techniques like TCP/IP stack fingerprinting and analysis of responses to crafted probes provide clues about the OS in use. This information assists ethical hackers in tailoring their attacks to the target's specific OS.

Network mapping is a critical component of network scanning, allowing ethical hackers to create a map or diagram of the target network's topology. Network mapping techniques involve identifying routers, switches, and other network devices, as well as their interconnections. This knowledge helps ethical hackers understand the network's layout and design.

Vulnerability scanning is an integral part of network scanning methods, as it focuses on identifying known vulnerabilities in the services or systems detected during the scan. Vulnerability scanners, such as Nessus, OpenVAS, and Qualys, automate the process of comparing software versions and configurations against a database of known vulnerabilities. This enables ethical hackers to generate comprehensive reports of potential weaknesses.

Network scanning also includes subnet enumeration and discovery techniques. These methods involve identifying subnets, IP ranges, and network segments within the target network. Subnet enumeration helps ethical hackers understand the network's organization and identify potential entry points for further assessments.

Intrusive scanning techniques, such as intrusive vulnerability scanning and exploitation testing, go beyond passive enumeration and actively probe for vulnerabilities that may lead to compromise. While these techniques can be effective in identifying weaknesses, they should be conducted with caution and proper authorization, as they may disrupt target systems or trigger alarms.

During network scanning, ethical hackers must exercise discretion and follow responsible disclosure practices. Scanning a network without proper authorization is not only unethical but also illegal in many jurisdictions. Therefore, it's essential to obtain explicit permission before conducting any network scanning activities.

Network scanning should be conducted systematically and with a clear plan in mind. Ethical hackers often create scanning profiles or scripts that outline the scanning techniques, target IP ranges, and goals of the scan. This structured approach ensures that all aspects of the network are thoroughly examined.

When performing network scanning, it's vital to prioritize scanning activities based on the network's critical assets and potential risks. Focus on high-value targets and sensitive systems first, as these are likely to have the greatest impact on security.

Detailed record-keeping is essential during network scanning. Ethical hackers should maintain logs of scan results, including open ports, services, operating system details, and identified vulnerabilities. These records serve as a reference for subsequent phases of ethical hacking, such as vulnerability assessment and exploitation.

In summary, network scanning methods are a cornerstone of ethical hacking, providing valuable insights into network structures, services, and potential vulnerabilities. These methods encompass port scanning, banner grabbing, operating system fingerprinting, network mapping, vulnerability scanning, subnet enumeration, and intrusion testing. Ethical hackers must conduct network scanning responsibly, with proper authorization and a focus on minimizing disruption to the target. By employing these techniques effectively, ethical hackers contribute to enhanced network security and the identification of vulnerabilities that can be addressed to strengthen cybersecurity.

Service enumeration techniques are a crucial part of

ethical hacking, helping professionals identify the specific services running on target systems. By understanding the services in operation, ethical hackers can assess potential vulnerabilities, misconfigurations, and entry points for further evaluation. Service enumeration involves systematically gathering information about the services, including their types, versions, and configurations.

One of the primary objectives of service enumeration is to determine the types of services that are running on target systems. This includes identifying whether services are web-based, database-related, email-related, file sharing, or other types of services. Each service type may have its own set of vulnerabilities and security considerations.

Banner grabbing is a common technique used in service enumeration. It involves connecting to open ports on target systems and retrieving banners or headers from the services. These banners often contain information about the service, including its name, version, and sometimes additional details that can be useful for further assessment.

Another service enumeration technique is to interact with services to gather information about their configuration and behavior. Ethical hackers may send specific requests or commands to services to elicit responses that reveal details about their settings or capabilities. This can include querying a web server for its supported HTTP methods or a database server for its supported protocols.

Service fingerprinting is an essential aspect of service enumeration. It involves identifying services based on unique characteristics or signatures. Fingerprinting techniques can be used to detect specific services, even when they are running on non-standard ports or have been configured to hide their identity.

Operating system detection is often combined with service enumeration to gain a more comprehensive understanding of the target system. By analyzing responses from services and examining patterns in the network traffic, ethical hackers can infer the underlying operating system in use.

Port scanning is closely related to service enumeration, as it helps identify open ports where services are listening. By scanning for open ports on target systems, ethical hackers can create a list of ports to investigate during service enumeration.

Service enumeration is not limited to external targets; it is equally valuable for internal network assessments. Ethical hackers can apply the same techniques to identify services running on internal servers and workstations, helping organizations maintain robust security both externally and internally.

Active and passive service enumeration techniques exist. Active techniques involve sending requests or probes to services, actively interacting with them to gather information. Passive techniques, on the other hand, rely on observing network traffic or analyzing existing data to infer the presence of services without direct interaction.

Enumerating services responsibly is a fundamental principle in ethical hacking. Ethical hackers should always obtain proper authorization to perform service enumeration activities on target systems, whether they are external or internal. Unauthorized scanning or probing can disrupt services and lead to unintended consequences.

Service enumeration should be performed systematically and documented thoroughly. Ethical hackers maintain records of the services identified, their versions, configurations, and any additional details that may be relevant for vulnerability assessment and subsequent phases of ethical hacking.

Understanding the services running on target systems is a crucial step in the ethical hacking process. It allows ethical hackers to tailor their assessments to the specific services in use, identify potential vulnerabilities, and prioritize security measures accordingly.

In summary, service enumeration techniques are essential tools in the arsenal of ethical hackers, enabling them to identify and understand the services running on target systems. These techniques encompass banner grabbing, interacting with services, fingerprinting, operating system detection, port scanning, and both active and passive approaches. Ethical hackers must conduct service enumeration responsibly, with proper authorization and a focus on gathering accurate and relevant information for vulnerability assessment and security improvement. By employing these techniques effectively, ethical hackers contribute to enhanced cybersecurity and the identification of potential risks.

Chapter 7: Exploitation Techniques for Beginners

Basic exploitation concepts are fundamental principles in the field of ethical hacking, as they form the basis for identifying and leveraging vulnerabilities to gain unauthorized access or control over target systems. Understanding these concepts is essential for ethical hackers to assess and secure systems effectively while simulating real-world attack scenarios.

One of the primary concepts in exploitation is the identification of vulnerabilities. Vulnerabilities are weaknesses or flaws in software, systems, or configurations that can be exploited by malicious actors to compromise the security of a target. These vulnerabilities can range from simple coding errors to misconfigurations or design flaws.

Exploits are software programs or techniques specifically designed to take advantage of vulnerabilities. Exploits leverage the weaknesses in a system or application to gain unauthorized access, execute arbitrary code, or manipulate the target in a way that benefits the attacker. Ethical hackers often use exploits to test the security of systems and identify areas that require improvement.

Privilege escalation is a key concept in exploitation, involving the escalation of user privileges to gain increased access or control over a target system. Privilege escalation exploits typically aim to elevate a user's privileges from a low-privilege account to a higher-privilege account, such as gaining administrative or root access.

Buffer overflows are a common vulnerability that plays a significant role in exploitation. A buffer overflow occurs when a program writes more data to a memory buffer than it can hold, leading to unintended consequences such as code execution or unauthorized access. Ethical hackers often use buffer overflow exploits to take control of a target system.

Code injection is another critical concept in exploitation, involving the insertion of malicious code into a system or application to manipulate its behavior. Common forms of code injection include SQL injection, where malicious SQL queries are injected into a web application to access or modify a database, and cross-site scripting (XSS), which allows attackers to inject malicious scripts into web pages viewed by other users.

Zero-day vulnerabilities are vulnerabilities that are not publicly known and have no official patches or fixes available. Exploiting zero-day vulnerabilities can be highly effective, as there are no known defenses against them. Ethical hackers may discover and report zero-day vulnerabilities to organizations or use them responsibly to assess a system's security.

Payloads are pieces of code or data that are delivered as part of an exploit to achieve a specific outcome. Payloads can range from simple commands to more complex scripts or programs. Ethical hackers often craft payloads to execute actions such as opening a remote shell, uploading or downloading files, or carrying out reconnaissance activities.

Exploitation techniques can be categorized into remote and local exploits. Remote exploits target vulnerabilities on remote systems accessible over a network, while local exploits target vulnerabilities that require physical or local access to the target system. Ethical hackers use both types of exploits to assess the security of systems effectively.

Social engineering is an essential concept in exploitation, as it involves manipulating individuals or users to divulge sensitive information or perform actions that aid an attacker. Social engineering attacks can range from phishing emails to impersonation tactics, and they often play a role in successful exploitation.

Payload obfuscation is a technique used to hide the true nature of a payload or exploit, making it more challenging for security defenses to detect and block. Ethical hackers may use payload obfuscation to evade intrusion detection systems and antivirus solutions.

Exploitation is a crucial phase in ethical hacking, but it must be conducted responsibly and with proper authorization. Unauthorized or malicious exploitation can lead to harm, legal consequences, or damage to systems and data. Ethical hackers must adhere to ethical guidelines and obtain explicit permission before attempting any exploitation activities.

In summary, basic exploitation concepts form the foundation for ethical hacking, enabling professionals to identify and leverage vulnerabilities to assess system security effectively. These concepts include vulnerabilities, exploits, privilege escalation, buffer overflows, code injection, zero-day vulnerabilities, payloads, remote and local exploits, social engineering, and payload obfuscation. Ethical hackers play a vital role in identifying and addressing security weaknesses to improve overall cybersecurity.

Practical exploitation examples provide valuable insights into how vulnerabilities can be leveraged in real-world scenarios, shedding light on the techniques ethical hackers use to assess and secure systems effectively. These examples illustrate the concepts of exploitation in action and demonstrate the importance of identifying and mitigating vulnerabilities.

One common practical exploitation example involves a web application vulnerable to SQL injection. In this scenario, an ethical hacker identifies a web form that accepts user input and doesn't properly validate or sanitize it. By crafting a malicious SQL query and injecting it into the input field, the hacker can manipulate the database backend, potentially gaining unauthorized access to sensitive information.

Another practical example is a buffer overflow vulnerability in a network service. Ethical hackers discover that a service running on a server doesn't adequately check the length of input data it receives. By sending specially crafted data, the hacker can overflow the buffer and execute arbitrary code on the target system, potentially taking control of it.

A classic exploitation scenario involves gaining unauthorized access to a network through weak or default credentials. Ethical hackers often find systems or devices with default usernames and passwords still in use. By leveraging these credentials, they can gain entry to the target network, emphasizing the importance of proper credential management.

Privilege escalation is a critical aspect of exploitation, and practical examples often involve elevating user privileges.

For instance, an ethical hacker may discover a vulnerable service running with low-privilege credentials. By exploiting a weakness, such as a misconfiguration or vulnerability, the hacker can escalate their privileges to gain administrative access.

Web application vulnerabilities, such as cross-site scripting (XSS), are prevalent in practical exploitation examples. In an XSS scenario, an ethical hacker identifies a web application that doesn't properly validate user inputs. By injecting malicious scripts, the hacker can manipulate the behavior of the web application and potentially steal user data or perform actions on behalf of users.

Zero-day vulnerabilities are of particular interest in practical exploitation. Ethical hackers may come across a vulnerability that has no known patches or fixes. In such cases, they carefully craft exploits to leverage these vulnerabilities while adhering to responsible disclosure practices.

Payloads play a crucial role in exploitation examples, as they are used to deliver malicious code or actions to the target system. Ethical hackers often create payloads to achieve specific objectives, such as gaining remote shell access or executing reconnaissance activities.

Social engineering tactics are prevalent in practical exploitation examples, highlighting the human element in cybersecurity. For instance, an ethical hacker might impersonate a trusted individual or organization to manipulate a user into revealing sensitive information or performing actions that benefit the attacker.

Practical exploitation examples emphasize the importance of thorough testing and validation of security measures. Ethical hackers simulate real-world attack scenarios to identify vulnerabilities and weaknesses that might otherwise go unnoticed.

It's crucial to recognize that ethical hackers operate within strict ethical and legal boundaries. They seek proper authorization before conducting exploitation activities and aim to improve cybersecurity rather than harm systems or data.

Exploitation examples provide a valuable learning opportunity for security professionals and organizations. By understanding how vulnerabilities can be exploited, they can better protect their systems and data.

In summary, practical exploitation examples illustrate the concepts and techniques of exploitation in the context of ethical hacking. These examples cover a range of scenarios, from web application vulnerabilities to privilege escalation and zero-day exploits. Ethical hackers use these examples to identify and address vulnerabilities, ultimately contributing to improved cybersecurity and the protection of systems and data.

Chapter 8: Reporting Vulnerabilities Effectively

Writing clear and detailed reports is a critical skill for ethical hackers and cybersecurity professionals, as it serves as the primary means of communicating findings, vulnerabilities, and recommendations to stakeholders.

Effective reporting begins with organizing information in a logical and structured manner, ensuring that the report flows coherently from start to finish.

The report's introduction should provide context, briefly outlining the scope of the assessment, the objectives, and any relevant background information.

Next, the report should describe the methodology used during the assessment, explaining the tools, techniques, and procedures employed to identify vulnerabilities and assess security.

When detailing vulnerabilities, it's essential to provide clear and concise descriptions, including the name, severity, and potential impact of each vulnerability.

Accurate and comprehensive technical details are crucial, as they enable readers to understand the vulnerabilities thoroughly and replicate the findings.

In addition to technical details, consider including screenshots, logs, or other evidence to support the findings and help stakeholders visualize the issues.

It's important to categorize vulnerabilities based on their severity, potential impact, and likelihood of exploitation, as this helps prioritize remediation efforts.

Providing recommendations for mitigating vulnerabilities is a crucial part of the report. These recommendations should be actionable, specific, and tailored to the organization's environment and resources.

Recommendations should also include a clear timeline for implementation and any associated risks if the vulnerabilities are not addressed promptly.

In some cases, ethical hackers may suggest compensating controls or alternative security measures to address vulnerabilities when immediate fixes are not feasible.

In addition to technical details, consider including a non-technical executive summary that provides a high-level overview of the findings, risks, and recommended actions.

The executive summary is particularly useful for stakeholders who may not have in-depth technical knowledge but need to understand the report's key takeaways.

When writing the report, use plain language and avoid technical jargon or acronyms that may be unfamiliar to the target audience.

Consider the report's audience, tailoring the level of technical detail to match the knowledge and expertise of the readers.

Ethical hackers should maintain objectivity and professionalism throughout the report, focusing on the facts and evidence rather than making subjective judgments or assumptions.

When documenting vulnerabilities, it's essential to include steps to reproduce the issues, allowing the organization's IT or security team to verify the findings independently.

Including a summary of the testing environment and any limitations or constraints that may have affected the assessment's scope or results adds transparency to the report.

Ethical hackers should take care to protect sensitive information and avoid disclosing any confidential or proprietary data in the report.

It's a best practice to obtain permission from the organization before sharing the report with external parties, ensuring that sensitive information remains confidential.

The report's conclusion should summarize the key findings, recommendations, and any potential next steps or actions required from the organization.

Proofreading and editing the report is essential to ensure clarity, accuracy, and professionalism. Typos, grammatical errors, or formatting issues can detract from the report's impact.

Ethical hackers should deliver the report to the organization promptly, maintaining open communication throughout the process and addressing any questions or concerns from the organization's stakeholders.

In some cases, ethical hackers may be required to present the findings in person to the organization's leadership or technical teams, providing an opportunity for further discussion and clarification.

After delivering the report, ethical hackers should follow up with the organization to ensure that the recommended actions are being implemented and that vulnerabilities are being addressed effectively.

In summary, writing clear and detailed reports is an essential skill for ethical hackers, enabling them to communicate findings, vulnerabilities, and recommendations effectively to organizations. These reports should be well-organized, include technical details, categorize vulnerabilities by severity, provide actionable recommendations, and consider the needs of the target audience. Ethical hackers should maintain professionalism, protect sensitive information, and follow up to ensure that recommended actions are taken. Clear and well-written reports are a valuable contribution to improving cybersecurity and mitigating risks.

Ethical responsibility in reporting is a cornerstone of the ethical hacking profession, emphasizing the importance of honesty, integrity, and transparency in the communication of findings, vulnerabilities, and recommendations.
Ethical hackers have a duty to act responsibly and ethically throughout the assessment process, from the initial scoping and engagement with the organization to the final reporting and follow-up stages.
One of the fundamental ethical responsibilities is obtaining proper authorization before conducting any assessment or penetration testing. This authorization ensures that ethical hackers have permission to assess the target systems and that their activities are lawful and within the organization's policies.
Ethical hackers must maintain strict confidentiality and protect sensitive information obtained during the assessment. This includes not disclosing confidential or proprietary data, trade secrets, or any information that could harm the organization.
Honesty is a core ethical principle, and ethical hackers should report findings truthfully, accurately, and without exaggeration or sensationalism. Avoiding the temptation to overstate or inflate the severity of vulnerabilities is essential to maintain credibility.

Integrity plays a crucial role in ethical responsibility. Ethical hackers should not engage in any activities that could compromise the integrity of the assessment or the organization's systems, such as planting backdoors or conducting malicious actions.

Transparency is another vital aspect of ethical responsibility. Ethical hackers should be open and transparent with the organization about the assessment process, objectives, and methodologies used.

When reporting vulnerabilities, ethical hackers should provide clear and detailed information, including technical details, evidence, and steps to reproduce the issues. Transparency ensures that the organization can validate the findings independently.

Ethical hackers should categorize vulnerabilities based on severity, potential impact, and likelihood of exploitation. This helps organizations prioritize their remediation efforts effectively.

Providing actionable recommendations is a key ethical responsibility. Ethical hackers should offer practical and feasible solutions for mitigating vulnerabilities, considering the organization's resources and constraints.

Recommendations should include a clear timeline for implementation and any associated risks if vulnerabilities are not addressed promptly. Ethical hackers should be realistic about the organization's capacity to implement recommendations.

Ethical hackers should refrain from making subjective judgments or assumptions in their reports. Stick to the facts and evidence, avoiding personal opinions or biases.

Maintaining objectivity throughout the reporting process is crucial, as it ensures that the assessment remains focused on identifying vulnerabilities and improving security rather than pursuing personal agendas.

In some cases, ethical hackers may discover zero-day vulnerabilities—vulnerabilities that have no known patches or fixes. Ethical responsibility dictates that these vulnerabilities should be handled with care and reported to the organization promptly.

Responsible disclosure is a critical aspect of ethical responsibility. Ethical hackers should work with the organization to develop a responsible disclosure plan, which may involve notifying the vendor or relevant authorities and giving them adequate time to address the vulnerabilities.

Ethical hackers should not publicly disclose vulnerabilities or exploit code until the organization has had a reasonable opportunity to address the issues. Premature disclosure can put the organization at risk and may not be in the best interest of security.

Respect for the organization's policies and procedures is essential. Ethical hackers should adhere to the organization's rules and guidelines throughout the assessment, reporting, and remediation processes.

Ethical responsibility extends beyond the reporting phase. Ethical hackers should follow up with the organization to ensure that the recommended actions are being implemented effectively and that vulnerabilities are being addressed.

Maintaining open and honest communication with the organization is essential, allowing for the exchange of information and updates throughout the remediation process.

In summary, ethical responsibility in reporting is a fundamental aspect of the ethical hacking profession. It emphasizes the importance of obtaining proper authorization, maintaining confidentiality, reporting findings truthfully, providing clear and detailed information, offering actionable recommendations, and following responsible disclosure practices. Ethical hackers have a duty to act with honesty, integrity, and transparency throughout the assessment and reporting process, ultimately contributing to improved cybersecurity and the protection of organizations' systems and data.

Chapter 9: Bug Fixing and Patch Management

Understanding the patching process is crucial for maintaining the security and stability of computer systems and software applications.

Patching involves the process of updating or fixing vulnerabilities, bugs, or issues in software, operating systems, or firmware.

These updates, often referred to as patches or security updates, are essential to address known vulnerabilities and improve the overall performance of the software.

Patching is a proactive measure taken by software vendors or developers to enhance the security and functionality of their products.

Vulnerabilities in software can be exploited by malicious actors to compromise systems, steal sensitive data, or disrupt operations.

Patching is a fundamental practice in cybersecurity, as it helps prevent security breaches and keeps systems protected against known threats.

Software vendors release patches in response to the discovery of security vulnerabilities or the identification of software bugs.

These patches are designed to fix specific issues or weaknesses in the software and are distributed to users through various channels.

One common way to receive patches is through automatic updates provided by operating systems or software applications.

These automatic updates can be configured to download and install patches as soon as they become available, ensuring that systems remain up-to-date and secure.

In addition to automatic updates, users can also manually download and install patches from official sources, such as the vendor's website or software repository.

The patching process typically begins with the identification of a security vulnerability or a software bug.

Vulnerabilities are often discovered through various means, including security research, penetration testing, or reports from users who have encountered issues.

Once a vulnerability is identified, the software vendor or developer assesses its severity and potential impact on users.

Vendors prioritize the release of patches based on factors such as the criticality of the vulnerability and the risk it poses to users.

Once a patch is developed, it undergoes rigorous testing to ensure that it effectively addresses the identified vulnerability without introducing new issues.

Testing includes evaluating the patch's compatibility with different configurations, systems, and environments to minimize the risk of causing unintended problems.

After successful testing, the patch is ready for release to users.

Software vendors typically announce the availability of patches through security advisories, release notes, or notifications within the software application.

Users are encouraged to apply patches promptly to protect their systems from potential threats.

Applying patches in a timely manner is essential because malicious actors may attempt to exploit vulnerabilities shortly after they become publicly known.

Patching is not limited to operating systems; it also applies to various software applications, including web browsers, office suites, and third-party software.

Third-party software vendors may release their own patches to address vulnerabilities or bugs in their products.

Organizations often have patch management policies and procedures in place to ensure that patches are applied consistently and efficiently across their IT infrastructure.

Patch management involves the planning, testing, deployment, and monitoring of patches to minimize disruption to operations.

In enterprise environments, patches may be deployed to a subset of systems or devices for testing before being rolled out to the entire organization.

Patch management tools and solutions are available to help organizations automate the process of deploying patches to multiple systems.

These tools can help ensure that patches are applied consistently and that systems remain protected.

In addition to security patches, software vendors may release updates that include new features, performance improvements, or bug fixes.

Users can choose to install these updates based on their specific needs and priorities.

It's important to note that while patching is a critical aspect of cybersecurity, it is not the sole solution to security threats.

Other security measures, such as firewall configurations, intrusion detection systems, and user education, complement patching to create a robust security posture.

In summary, understanding the patching process is essential for maintaining the security and functionality of computer systems and software applications.

Patching involves the identification and remediation of vulnerabilities and software bugs through the deployment of updates or patches.

These updates are released by software vendors in response to identified issues and are essential for protecting systems against known threats.

Users can receive patches through automatic updates or by manually downloading and installing them from official sources.

Patch management policies and procedures help organizations apply patches consistently and efficiently to minimize security risks.

While patching is a critical cybersecurity practice, it is just one component of a comprehensive security strategy that includes various measures to safeguard systems and data.

Navigating the landscape of bug mitigation presents various challenges for organizations and security professionals alike. These challenges are inherent in the process of identifying, addressing, and resolving software vulnerabilities that could potentially be exploited by malicious actors.

One of the primary challenges in bug mitigation is the ever-evolving nature of software vulnerabilities. As software systems and applications continue to advance, new types of vulnerabilities emerge regularly, making it essential for security teams to stay updated and vigilant.

Furthermore, the complexity of modern software poses a significant challenge. Software can consist of numerous components, libraries, and dependencies, each with its own potential vulnerabilities. Identifying and mitigating these vulnerabilities requires a comprehensive understanding of the entire software stack.

The rapid pace of software development, driven by the demand for new features and functionality, can lead to rushed code releases. In such cases, thorough security testing and vulnerability assessments may be overlooked, increasing the likelihood of undiscovered bugs.

Bug mitigation efforts may also face challenges related to resource constraints. Organizations may have limited time, personnel, or financial resources dedicated to security, making it difficult to address vulnerabilities promptly and effectively.

Prioritization is a key challenge in bug mitigation. Security teams often encounter numerous vulnerabilities, and determining which ones pose the greatest risk and should be addressed first can be a complex task.

Additionally, false positives in vulnerability scanning and assessment tools can lead to wasted time and resources, as security teams investigate and attempt to mitigate non-existent vulnerabilities.

The coordination and communication required for bug mitigation can also be challenging. Effective collaboration between development and security teams is essential to ensure that vulnerabilities are identified, reported, and resolved efficiently.

In some cases, the responsible disclosure of vulnerabilities can be challenging. Security researchers and ethical hackers who discover vulnerabilities may face obstacles when attempting to report their findings to organizations, hindering the mitigation process.

Another challenge is the presence of legacy systems and software within organizations. These systems may be difficult to patch or update, leaving them vulnerable to known exploits.

The diversity of software environments and platforms further complicates bug mitigation efforts. Organizations may have a mix of on-premises, cloud-based, and mobile applications, each requiring a tailored approach to vulnerability management.

The rise of Internet of Things (IoT) devices presents unique challenges in bug mitigation. IoT devices often lack robust security features and may be challenging to patch or update, making them susceptible to exploitation.

Furthermore, the growing sophistication of cyberattacks and threat actors adds complexity to bug mitigation. Attackers continuously adapt and develop new techniques, making it crucial for security teams to anticipate and respond to emerging threats effectively.

Legal and compliance considerations also play a role in bug mitigation. Organizations may be subject to regulations that require them to disclose and address vulnerabilities promptly, adding a layer of complexity to the process.

In some cases, bug mitigation efforts can inadvertently introduce new issues or disrupt operations. Patching vulnerabilities without proper testing and validation can lead to system instability or compatibility problems.

Lastly, the human factor is a significant challenge in bug mitigation. Security awareness and education are critical for all employees to reduce the risk of human error that could lead to the exploitation of vulnerabilities.

In summary, bug mitigation is a complex and multifaceted process that presents various challenges for organizations and security professionals. These challenges include the evolving nature of vulnerabilities, software complexity, resource constraints, prioritization, false positives, coordination, responsible disclosure, legacy systems, diverse environments, IoT devices, cyber threats, legal considerations, unintended consequences, and the human factor. Successfully addressing these challenges requires a proactive and holistic approach to security that encompasses prevention, detection, and response measures.

Chapter 10: Continuous Learning and Advancing Your Skills

Staying updated in the field of technology and cybersecurity is crucial to remain effective and competitive in this dynamic and ever-evolving industry. It's like keeping your toolkit sharp and your skills finely tuned to tackle new challenges and opportunities that arise regularly.

In today's fast-paced tech landscape, new developments, threats, and trends emerge continuously. Therefore, cybersecurity professionals must adopt a proactive approach to learning and staying informed.

One effective way to stay updated is by regularly reading industry news and publications. There are numerous online resources, blogs, and magazines dedicated to technology and cybersecurity, where experts share insights, research findings, and the latest updates. Keeping an eye on these sources is like having a constant stream of knowledge at your fingertips.

Conferences and seminars are excellent opportunities to gain firsthand knowledge from experts and peers. Attending industry events allows you to network, exchange ideas, and learn about cutting-edge technologies and best practices. It's a bit like attending a workshop where you can interact with the best minds in the field.

Online courses and training programs are readily available, covering a wide range of cybersecurity topics. These courses offer flexible learning options, allowing you to acquire new skills and knowledge at your own pace.

They're akin to having a personal mentor guiding you through the latest advancements.

Engaging in professional organizations and communities can be highly beneficial. These groups provide a platform for networking, sharing experiences, and learning from others. It's like joining a club of like-minded individuals who are passionate about staying ahead in the field.

Certifications are valuable for enhancing your skills and validating your expertise. Many organizations offer certification programs that cover various cybersecurity domains. Earning certifications is akin to earning badges that showcase your proficiency to employers and peers.

Becoming a member of industry forums and discussion groups can provide valuable insights. Participating in these forums allows you to ask questions, share your knowledge, and learn from the experiences of others. It's a bit like being part of a friendly community where everyone helps each other grow.

Podcasts and webinars are excellent mediums for consuming content on the go. You can listen to industry experts discuss current topics and trends while commuting, exercising, or doing household chores. It's like having your own personal radio show tailored to your interests.

Mentorship is a powerful way to stay updated and grow in your career. Connecting with a mentor who has extensive experience in the field can provide invaluable guidance, share practical insights, and help you navigate your professional journey. It's like having a wise and experienced friend by your side.

Hands-on experience is essential for mastering new skills and technologies. Creating a lab environment or volunteering for real-world projects can give you practical exposure to the latest tools and techniques. It's akin to learning to ride a bike by actually getting on one and pedaling.

Continuous learning and curiosity are the cornerstones of staying updated in the field. The tech and cybersecurity landscape will keep evolving, and embracing a mindset of lifelong learning will help you adapt and thrive. It's like embarking on an exciting adventure where each new discovery leads to another.

In summary, staying updated in the field of technology and cybersecurity is a dynamic and ongoing process. It involves a combination of reading, attending events, taking courses, engaging with communities, earning certifications, finding mentors, gaining hands-on experience, and maintaining a curious mindset. By staying informed and continuously improving your skills, you can remain at the forefront of the industry and contribute to a safer digital world.

Mentoring and skill enhancement are integral aspects of personal and professional growth, akin to having a guiding star that helps you navigate your journey toward becoming a better version of yourself.

Mentoring, in essence, is a symbiotic relationship where a more experienced individual, the mentor, shares their knowledge, wisdom, and insights with a less experienced person, the mentee, in a spirit of guidance and support.

Mentors serve as trusted advisors, offering valuable perspectives and advice based on their own experiences, much like a compass helping you find your way in a new and unfamiliar terrain.

One of the primary benefits of mentoring is knowledge transfer. Mentors can impart knowledge that may not be readily available in textbooks or formal training, offering a more practical and nuanced understanding of a subject.

Skills enhancement is an essential part of professional development, like refining a craft through practice and dedication. It involves acquiring new skills, improving existing ones, and staying updated with the latest industry trends.

A mentor can provide personalized guidance to help mentees identify their strengths and weaknesses, allowing them to focus their skill enhancement efforts effectively, similar to a personal coach tailoring workouts to an athlete's abilities.

Mentors often serve as role models, demonstrating the importance of ethics, professionalism, and continuous learning, much like a lighthouse guiding ships safely through rough waters.

Mentoring is not limited to technical skills; it can encompass various aspects of personal and professional development, including communication, leadership, time management, and problem-solving skills.

Skill enhancement requires dedication and a growth mindset. Individuals who actively seek opportunities for improvement and are open to feedback are more likely to succeed in their skill development journey.

Mentors can provide valuable feedback and constructive criticism to help mentees identify areas where they can enhance their skills, much like a coach offering guidance on refining a sports technique.

Skill enhancement often involves setting specific goals and benchmarks to measure progress, similar to a roadmap that guides you toward your desired destination.

Mentoring can provide accountability and motivation, helping mentees stay committed to their skill enhancement goals, much like a workout partner who encourages you to keep pushing your limits.

Effective mentors create a supportive and nurturing environment where mentees feel safe to ask questions, make mistakes, and experiment with new ideas, akin to a gardener providing the right conditions for plants to thrive.

In the digital age, online mentoring platforms and communities have emerged, providing opportunities for individuals to connect with mentors from around the world, expanding their horizons like a global network of mentors.

Skill enhancement often involves seeking out learning opportunities, such as workshops, courses, webinars, and tutorials, to acquire new knowledge and practical skills, similar to attending classes at a university.

Mentors can help mentees identify the most relevant and valuable learning resources, saving them time and effort in their skill enhancement journey.

Personalized guidance from a mentor can accelerate skill enhancement by focusing on the areas that will have the most significant impact on a mentee's goals, similar to a tailor crafting a custom-fit suit.

Mentoring relationships can be formal or informal, structured or flexible, depending on the needs and preferences of both the mentor and mentee, like different styles of coaching in sports.

Skill enhancement often involves continuous practice and repetition to master a skill, much like a musician practicing scales to improve their playing.

A mentor can provide mentees with real-world insights and practical tips that may not be found in textbooks or online courses, offering a more holistic understanding of a subject.

Mentoring is a two-way street, as mentors also benefit from the relationship by gaining a sense of fulfillment and personal growth through helping others, much like a teacher who learns from their students.

Skill enhancement can lead to increased confidence and competence in one's abilities, empowering individuals to tackle new challenges and opportunities with enthusiasm, akin to a well-prepared explorer venturing into uncharted territory.

In summary, mentoring and skill enhancement are intertwined aspects of personal and professional development that provide guidance, support, and opportunities for growth. Mentors offer valuable insights and knowledge, akin to a guiding star or compass, while skill enhancement involves acquiring and refining skills through dedication, practice, and learning opportunities. Both mentoring and skill enhancement contribute to an individual's journey toward becoming a more knowledgeable, competent, and confident version of themselves.

BOOK 2
INTERMEDIATE BUG HUNTING TECHNIQUES
FROM NOVICE TO SKILLED HUNTER

ROB BOTWRIGHT

Chapter 1: Building on the Basics: A Review for Novices

Revisiting fundamentals is a valuable practice in any field, serving as a reminder of the foundational principles that underpin more advanced concepts and techniques.

Imagine the fundamentals as the building blocks upon which a solid understanding of any subject is constructed, much like the sturdy foundation of a well-built house.

In the realm of technology and cybersecurity, revisiting fundamentals is akin to revisiting the basics of mathematics before diving into complex calculus.

Fundamentals in technology encompass a wide range of topics, from the basics of computer hardware and software to fundamental networking concepts.

Understanding the fundamentals of computer hardware, such as processors, memory, and storage, is like knowing the basic components of an engine in automotive engineering.

These hardware fundamentals provide a crucial foundation for comprehending how computers function and interact with software, just as understanding engine components is essential for designing and troubleshooting automotive systems.

Similarly, knowledge of operating systems and their core functions is fundamental in the world of technology, much like understanding the principles of mechanical engineering in building structures.

Operating systems act as the bridge between hardware and software, facilitating communication and resource management, similar to how structural engineering principles ensure the stability and functionality of buildings.

Fundamental networking concepts, such as IP addresses, protocols, and routing, are the backbone of modern connectivity, just as the concept of electricity is the backbone of electrical engineering.

Networking fundamentals enable data to flow seamlessly across the internet and within local networks, much like electricity powers electrical systems, from light bulbs to complex machinery.

In the realm of cybersecurity, revisiting the fundamentals is like revisiting the core principles of a martial art before mastering advanced techniques.

One of the most fundamental concepts in cybersecurity is the principle of confidentiality, ensuring that sensitive information remains private and protected, similar to the way a vault secures valuable assets.

Integrity, another fundamental cybersecurity principle, ensures the accuracy and trustworthiness of data, much like the integrity of a building's structure guarantees its stability.

Availability is another core principle, ensuring that systems and resources are accessible when needed, similar to how reliable utilities ensure a continuous supply of water and electricity.

Authentication and authorization, fundamental in cybersecurity, are like security checkpoints that verify identities and grant access only to authorized individuals, just as secure entry points restrict access to certain areas.

Understanding the fundamentals of encryption, such as symmetric and asymmetric cryptography, is akin to knowing the basic principles of locks and keys in physical security.

Encryption ensures that data remains secure during transmission and storage, similar to how locks safeguard physical belongings.

Fundamental cybersecurity concepts also include risk assessment and management, which are like the safety assessments carried out in construction projects to identify potential hazards and mitigate them.

By revisiting the fundamentals of cybersecurity, individuals can gain a deeper understanding of the core principles that guide the field, much like revisiting the foundational principles of ethics in any profession.

Ethical considerations in cybersecurity, such as privacy and consent, are fundamental to ensuring responsible and lawful practices, similar to ethical principles that guide medical professionals in their care for patients.

Revisiting the fundamentals of cybersecurity helps professionals make ethical decisions and navigate the complex landscape of technology and information security, much like revisiting the core values of honesty and integrity in personal relationships.

In summary, revisiting fundamentals is a valuable practice in technology and cybersecurity, providing a strong foundation for understanding complex concepts and making ethical and informed decisions. Just as the basics of mathematics, engineering, and ethics underpin advanced knowledge, the fundamentals of technology and cybersecurity are essential for professionals in these fields. By embracing the fundamentals, individuals can build a solid foundation for continuous learning and growth, ensuring their expertise remains grounded in core principles.

Practical exercises are a fantastic way for novices to apply what they've learned in a hands-on, real-world context, much like practicing a musical instrument to develop your skills further.

These exercises provide an opportunity to bridge the gap between theory and practice, allowing novices to gain valuable experience and confidence in their chosen field, similar to learning to drive a car by actually getting behind the wheel.

One of the fundamental exercises for novices in technology is setting up a virtual lab environment, which is akin to creating a safe and controlled space for experimentation and learning.

In this lab, novices can install and configure various software and operating systems, much like a chef experimenting with different ingredients to perfect a recipe.

By working in a virtual lab, novices can make mistakes and learn from them without the risk of damaging real-world systems, similar to a scientist conducting experiments in a controlled laboratory environment.

Another practical exercise for novices is troubleshooting common software and hardware issues, which is like solving puzzles to sharpen problem-solving skills.

By encountering and resolving real-world problems, novices gain confidence in their ability to diagnose and fix issues, much like a detective solving a case.

Building a basic website or web application is another valuable exercise for novices in the realm of technology, similar to a young artist starting with simple sketches to develop their artistic skills.

This exercise allows novices to apply their knowledge of web development languages and frameworks, providing a tangible result that showcases their progress and creativity.

Exploring coding challenges and online coding platforms is an excellent way for novices to practice programming skills, much like an athlete training regularly to improve their performance.

Coding challenges can range from simple tasks to complex problems, offering a gradual progression in difficulty and helping novices build their coding muscles.

Engaging in cybersecurity capture the flag (CTF) challenges is a fun and educational exercise for novices interested in cybersecurity, similar to playing strategic games to enhance problem-solving abilities.

CTF challenges involve solving puzzles and completing tasks related to hacking and security, allowing novices to develop their ethical hacking skills in a controlled environment.

Participating in open-source projects and contributing to collaborative coding efforts is a way for novices to gain practical experience while working with experienced developers, much like joining a team sport to improve teamwork and communication skills.

Open-source projects provide an opportunity to work on real-world coding projects, learn from mentors, and make valuable contributions to the tech community.

Practical exercises for novices extend beyond the realm of technology and into various fields. For those interested in writing, regularly composing short stories or articles can help improve writing skills, similar to a novelist practicing by writing daily.

Novices can also engage in language-learning exercises by conversing with native speakers or immersing themselves in a language-rich environment, much like travelers picking up a new language through daily interactions.

In the realm of science, conducting simple experiments or replicating famous scientific studies can help novices grasp fundamental scientific principles, similar to budding scientists conducting experiments to expand their knowledge.

In the world of art, novices can explore different techniques, such as sketching, painting, or sculpting, to develop their artistic abilities and express their creativity, akin to an artist experimenting with various mediums.

For novices interested in business and entrepreneurship, creating a small business plan or launching a micro-business can be a practical exercise to gain firsthand experience, much like an aspiring entrepreneur starting a small venture to learn the ropes.

Practical exercises for novices are not limited to specific fields but can encompass a wide range of interests and passions. They provide a hands-on, experiential learning opportunity that complements formal education and empowers novices to develop their skills and expertise.

These exercises offer a sense of accomplishment and progression, similar to leveling up in a video game or achieving milestones in a personal journey.

In summary, practical exercises for novices are invaluable for building skills, gaining experience, and boosting confidence in various fields, from technology and science to art and entrepreneurship. Just as athletes train to excel in their sport and musicians practice to master their instruments, novices can engage in practical exercises to develop their talents and pursue their passions. These exercises bridge the gap between theory and practice, empowering novices to apply what they've learned and take the first steps on their journey toward expertise.

Chapter 2: Deep Dive into Common Vulnerabilities

Understanding the OWASP Top 10 is essential for anyone involved in web application development and cybersecurity, much like understanding traffic rules is crucial for safe driving.

The OWASP Top 10 is a regularly updated list of the most critical web application security risks, serving as a guide for developers, security professionals, and organizations to prioritize and address these risks.

Think of the OWASP Top 10 as a security checklist that helps ensure web applications are protected against common vulnerabilities that could be exploited by malicious actors.

One of the top risks in the OWASP Top 10 is Injection, which is like a stealthy intruder gaining access to a secure building by manipulating the entry system.

Injection vulnerabilities occur when untrusted data is included in a command or query and executed unintentionally, allowing attackers to inject malicious code.

Another significant risk is Broken Authentication, akin to someone accessing your bank account because they discovered your PIN and password.

Broken Authentication vulnerabilities occur when authentication mechanisms are not properly implemented, enabling unauthorized users to gain access to sensitive data or perform actions on behalf of legitimate users.

Cross-Site Scripting (XSS) is another critical risk, similar to a con artist tricking someone into revealing personal information.

XSS vulnerabilities allow attackers to inject malicious scripts into web applications, which can then execute within a user's browser, potentially stealing user data or performing malicious actions.

Insecure Deserialization is a risk that involves an attacker exploiting weaknesses in the deserialization process, much like someone tampering with a package in transit to alter its contents.

This vulnerability can lead to remote code execution, allowing attackers to take control of the application or steal data.

Security Misconfiguration is a risk similar to leaving the door to a vault unlocked, as it involves improperly configured security settings that can expose sensitive information or grant unauthorized access.

Sensitive Data Exposure is akin to a classified document being left in an unlocked drawer, as it involves the exposure of sensitive information, such as passwords or credit card numbers.

Broken Access Control vulnerabilities allow attackers to access restricted resources or perform actions that should be prohibited, similar to someone bypassing a security checkpoint at an airport.

XML External Entity (XXE) attacks are like a hacker exploiting a hidden backdoor to gain unauthorized access to a system, as they involve manipulating XML input to disclose internal files or execute remote code.

Security components with known vulnerabilities are similar to a building with a weak foundation, as they can be exploited by attackers to gain access to an application or its data.

Insufficient Logging and Monitoring, the final risk on the OWASP Top 10, is like a security system that doesn't alert anyone when an intruder enters a building.

This risk involves the failure to log and monitor security events, making it challenging to detect and respond to security incidents effectively.

Understanding the OWASP Top 10 is crucial because it helps developers identify and mitigate these common vulnerabilities in their web applications, similar to knowing how to protect a house from common security risks.

By addressing these vulnerabilities, organizations can enhance the security of their web applications and reduce the risk of data breaches, financial losses, and damage to their reputation.

Furthermore, understanding the OWASP Top 10 is not only beneficial for developers but also for security professionals, as it provides a framework for assessing the security posture of web applications and guiding security testing efforts.

Organizations can use the OWASP Top 10 as a foundation for building a robust security program, ensuring that security is integrated into the software development lifecycle from the outset, rather than being treated as an afterthought.

By proactively addressing the risks outlined in the OWASP Top 10, organizations can minimize the likelihood of security incidents and their associated costs, such as legal liabilities and regulatory fines.

In summary, understanding the OWASP Top 10 is a fundamental step in enhancing the security of web applications and protecting sensitive data from malicious threats. Just as knowing common safety hazards is vital for maintaining a secure environment, knowledge of the OWASP Top 10 is essential for safeguarding web applications against prevalent security risks. By prioritizing security and implementing best practices, organizations can build resilient and secure web applications that stand up to the challenges of the digital age.

Real-world vulnerability examples illustrate the importance of understanding and mitigating security risks in today's digital landscape, akin to cautionary tales that highlight potential dangers in everyday life.

One notable real-world vulnerability is the Heartbleed bug, which is similar to a hidden flaw in a lock that exposes a building to unauthorized access.

Heartbleed was a serious security vulnerability in the widely used OpenSSL cryptographic software library, which is responsible for secure communication on the internet.

This vulnerability allowed attackers to read sensitive data from the memory of affected servers, potentially exposing passwords, private keys, and other confidential information.

The Equifax data breach is another compelling example, akin to a massive heist where valuable assets were stolen due to a security lapse.

In this incident, attackers exploited a vulnerability in Apache Struts, a widely used web application framework, to gain access to Equifax's database.

As a result, the personal and financial information of nearly 147 million individuals was compromised, leading to significant financial and reputational damage for the company.

The WannaCry ransomware attack serves as a stark reminder of the real-world consequences of unpatched vulnerabilities, much like a sudden and destructive storm wreaking havoc.

WannaCry exploited a vulnerability in Microsoft's Windows operating system, which had a patch available but was not applied to many affected systems.

This ransomware attack spread rapidly, encrypting data and demanding a ransom for its release, affecting organizations worldwide and causing widespread disruption.

The Meltdown and Spectre vulnerabilities are similar to stealthy spies infiltrating secure locations, as they exposed critical flaws in modern computer processors.

These vulnerabilities allowed attackers to potentially access sensitive data, including passwords and encryption keys, by exploiting the design of processors themselves.

The Apache Log4j vulnerability, known as Log4Shell, is like a hidden backdoor that allows unauthorized access to a secure facility.

This vulnerability, discovered in the widely used Log4j logging library, allowed attackers to execute arbitrary code on affected servers, potentially leading to data breaches and system compromise.

The SolarWinds cyberattack, reminiscent of an infiltration by a sophisticated spy agency, targeted the software supply chain, compromising trusted software updates distributed to numerous organizations.

Attackers inserted a malicious code into a software update for SolarWinds' Orion platform, granting them access to sensitive networks and information across various sectors.

The critical infrastructure attack on Colonial Pipeline demonstrated the real-world impact of vulnerabilities in industrial control systems, much like a breach in a dam threatening to flood a city.

In this case, ransomware attackers targeted the pipeline's control systems, causing a temporary shutdown and disruptions in fuel supply to the eastern United States.

The Log4j vulnerability, known as Log4Shell, is like a hidden backdoor that allows unauthorized access to a secure facility.

This vulnerability, discovered in the widely used Log4j logging library, allowed attackers to execute arbitrary code on affected servers, potentially leading to data breaches and system compromise.

These real-world vulnerability examples underscore the importance of proactive security measures, continuous monitoring, and timely patching of software and systems to mitigate potential risks, much like maintaining a building to prevent structural weaknesses.

They also highlight the need for organizations to stay vigilant and invest in cybersecurity measures to protect sensitive data and critical infrastructure, akin to fortifying defenses to withstand potential threats.

In summary, real-world vulnerability examples serve as cautionary tales that emphasize the critical importance of cybersecurity in today's interconnected digital world. Just as understanding common safety hazards is essential for personal safety, awareness of vulnerabilities and security best practices is crucial for protecting organizations and individuals from potential threats and attacks. By learning from these examples and implementing robust security measures, we can reduce the risks associated with vulnerabilities and create a safer digital environment for all.

Chapter 3: Advanced Scanning and Enumeration

Advanced port scanning techniques are a vital component of network reconnaissance and security assessments, much like a skilled detective using specialized tools to uncover hidden clues in a complex case.

These techniques go beyond basic port scanning to provide a deeper understanding of network services, vulnerabilities, and potential attack vectors.

One advanced port scanning technique is banner grabbing, which is akin to reading the signage on a storefront to understand the nature of a business.

Banner grabbing involves connecting to open ports and collecting information from the banners or banners that services display, revealing software versions and potentially vulnerable configurations.

Operating system fingerprinting is another technique, similar to identifying a person by their unique characteristics, such as fingerprints or facial features.

This method aims to determine the underlying operating system of a target system by analyzing subtle differences in how it responds to network requests.

The use of stealth scanning techniques, like a cat sneaking through the night, allows a scanner to minimize its footprint and avoid detection by intrusion detection systems (IDS) or firewalls.

Stealth scans include techniques such as TCP SYN scanning, TCP ACK scanning, and TCP window scanning, which send packets that are less likely to trigger alarms.

Idle scanning, also known as zombie scanning, involves using an intermediary system, or zombie, to scan a target system, making it challenging to trace the true source of the scan.

This technique can be useful for maintaining anonymity during scans and evading network defenses.

Advanced port scanning techniques also include the use of decoy hosts, similar to a diversion tactic in a military operation.

Decoy scanning involves sending packets to multiple hosts, including the target, to make it harder for defenders to distinguish between legitimate traffic and the scan.

Some scanning tools offer scripting capabilities, similar to a Swiss Army knife with various attachments for different tasks.

These scripts can automate complex scanning procedures and customize scan parameters, enhancing the efficiency and effectiveness of scans.

UDP scanning is another advanced technique, akin to exploring the less-traveled paths of a network.

Unlike TCP, which is connection-oriented, UDP is connectionless, making it challenging to scan. Advanced UDP scanning methods involve sending specialized packets to identify open UDP ports.

Vulnerability scanning can be considered an advanced port scanning extension, akin to a detective analyzing evidence to identify weaknesses.

Vulnerability scanners not only discover open ports but also assess the security of services running on those ports, identifying potential vulnerabilities that could be exploited.

Timing and rate control are critical aspects of advanced port scanning techniques, much like a musician adjusting the tempo and volume of a performance for the desired effect.

These controls allow scanners to fine-tune scan speeds and avoid overwhelming target systems or triggering security alerts.

Parallel scanning, similar to a team of investigators working on different aspects of a case simultaneously, involves scanning multiple targets or multiple ports on a single target in parallel.

This technique can significantly reduce the time required to complete comprehensive scans.

Using proxies is a method to mask the origin of a scan, similar to conducting an investigation through a confidential informant.

Proxies act as intermediaries between the scanning tool and the target, making it challenging for defenders to trace the source of the scan back to the attacker.

Advanced port scanning techniques often include evasion tactics, like a master thief avoiding security cameras and alarms.

These tactics involve crafting scan packets to bypass intrusion detection systems and firewalls, enabling scans to go undetected.

It's essential to consider ethical and legal implications when employing advanced port scanning techniques, similar to adhering to the rules and regulations governing investigative procedures.

Unauthorized or malicious scanning can lead to legal consequences and damage to an organization's reputation.

In summary, advanced port scanning techniques are a crucial part of network reconnaissance and security assessments, allowing professionals to gain a deeper understanding of network configurations and potential vulnerabilities. Like skilled investigators, practitioners of these techniques use specialized tools and methods to uncover valuable information while considering ethical and legal considerations. By mastering advanced port scanning, security professionals can better protect their organizations from potential threats and vulnerabilities, ensuring the safety and integrity of their networks.

Enumerating hidden services is a crucial aspect of cybersecurity, much like uncovering hidden treasures in a vast landscape.

Hidden services, also known as dark services, refer to services, applications, or systems that are intentionally concealed or not visible to typical network scans.

The need to enumerate hidden services arises from the fact that organizations may deploy critical infrastructure and resources in ways that are not immediately apparent, akin to hiding valuables in a secret compartment.

By enumerating hidden services, security professionals can gain insights into potential attack surfaces, vulnerabilities, and misconfigurations that may not be evident through standard network scans.

One common technique for enumerating hidden services is banner grabbing, which is akin to identifying a shop by the sign displayed at its entrance.

Banner grabbing involves connecting to open ports and collecting information from the banners or headers that services display, revealing details about software versions, configurations, and potentially exploitable vulnerabilities.

Operating system fingerprinting is another valuable technique for enumerating hidden services, much like identifying a person by their unique characteristics or mannerisms.

This method aims to determine the underlying operating system of a target system by analyzing subtle differences in how it responds to network requests.

Service enumeration often involves probing for open ports and services on a target system, similar to searching for hidden entrances or access points in a building.

Scanning tools like Nmap, with its extensive database of service fingerprints, can assist in identifying running services and their versions, providing valuable information for enumerating hidden services.

When enumerating hidden services, it's essential to employ stealthy scanning techniques, similar to a spy operating covertly in enemy territory.

Stealth scans, such as TCP SYN scanning or TCP ACK scanning, send packets that are less likely to trigger intrusion detection systems (IDS) or firewall alarms, allowing for discreet enumeration.

Idle scanning, also known as zombie scanning, involves using an intermediary system, or zombie, to scan a target system, making it challenging to trace the true source of the enumeration.

This technique can be advantageous for maintaining anonymity during scans and evading network defenses.

Advanced scanning techniques like decoy scanning can be valuable for enumerating hidden services, much like using diversions to distract attention.

Decoy scanning involves sending packets to multiple hosts, including the target, to confuse defenders and make it harder to distinguish between legitimate traffic and the enumeration.

Some scanning tools offer scripting capabilities, similar to using specialized tools for specific tasks, which can automate complex enumeration procedures and customize scan parameters.

Scripts can be tailored to discover hidden services and gather detailed information about them, enhancing the effectiveness of enumeration efforts.

UDP scanning is another essential technique when enumerating hidden services, akin to exploring less-traveled paths in search of hidden treasures.

Unlike TCP, which is connection-oriented, UDP is connectionless, making it challenging to scan. Advanced UDP scanning methods involve sending specialized packets to identify open UDP ports and discover hidden services.

Enumerating hidden services often extends beyond identifying open ports to uncovering valuable information about running applications and their configurations, similar to deciphering clues to unveil hidden secrets.

Vulnerability scanning can be considered an extension of service enumeration, as it not only discovers open ports but also assesses the security of services, identifying potential vulnerabilities that could be exploited.

The timing and rate control of enumeration scans are critical aspects, akin to adjusting the tempo and volume of a performance to achieve the desired effect.

These controls allow enumerators to fine-tune scan speeds, avoid overwhelming target systems, and reduce the risk of detection.

Parallel scanning, similar to teamwork in an investigation, involves scanning multiple targets or multiple ports on a single target in parallel.

This technique can significantly reduce the time required to complete comprehensive enumeration scans, increasing efficiency and coverage.

Proxies and anonymization techniques are valuable tools when enumerating hidden services, much like concealing one's identity when investigating sensitive matters.

Proxies act as intermediaries between the enumeration tool and the target, making it challenging for defenders to trace the source of the enumeration back to the enumerator.

Evasion tactics, similar to the strategies employed by stealthy operatives, are often necessary when enumerating hidden services.

These tactics involve crafting enumeration packets to bypass intrusion detection systems and firewalls, allowing scans to go undetected.

Enumerating hidden services requires a thorough understanding of networking protocols, service behaviors, and security technologies, similar to the expertise needed to decipher complex codes.

Ethical considerations are paramount when enumerating hidden services, much like the adherence to legal and ethical standards in any investigative endeavor.

Unauthorized or malicious enumeration can lead to legal consequences and damage to an organization's reputation.

In summary, enumerating hidden services is a critical aspect of cybersecurity, enabling professionals to uncover concealed resources, vulnerabilities, and potential risks.

Much like a detective unraveling a mystery, enumerating hidden services involves using specialized techniques and tools to reveal valuable insights. By mastering the art of enumeration, security professionals can enhance their ability to assess and protect networks effectively, safeguarding organizations from potential threats and vulnerabilities.

Chapter 4: Exploiting Complex Vulnerabilities

Advanced exploitation methods are the pinnacle of offensive cybersecurity, much like the sophisticated tactics employed by elite covert operatives in high-stakes missions.

These methods go beyond the basics of vulnerability discovery to leverage discovered weaknesses in intricate and strategic ways, making them essential for red teaming, penetration testing, and ethical hacking.

In the world of advanced exploitation, attackers often need to evade detection, bypass security mechanisms, and maintain persistence, similar to infiltrating a heavily guarded facility without raising alarm.

One advanced exploitation method is the use of zero-day exploits, which are akin to having a master key that can unlock previously unknown vulnerabilities.

Zero-days target flaws in software or hardware that are undisclosed and unpatched, giving attackers a significant advantage as defenders have no countermeasures in place.

Exploiting complex vulnerabilities, like a master locksmith manipulating intricate locks, requires in-depth knowledge of the target system's architecture and the ability to craft precise and customized exploits.

These vulnerabilities often involve multiple layers of complexity, making them challenging to identify and exploit.

Privilege escalation is a critical aspect of advanced exploitation, similar to gaining access to restricted areas by impersonating a high-ranking official.

This technique involves elevating one's privileges within a compromised system to gain increased control and access to sensitive resources.

Post-exploitation is like the covert operations that follow a successful infiltration, as it involves maintaining access, collecting intelligence, and potentially pivoting to other systems.

Effective post-exploitation techniques allow attackers to operate undetected and achieve their objectives.

Web application security assessment is a specialized field within advanced exploitation, much like a safe-cracker focusing on intricate vaults.

Advanced web application exploitation techniques involve manipulating web applications to gain unauthorized access or control, often exploiting complex vulnerabilities like SQL injection or remote code execution.

Network security and infrastructure testing are crucial components of advanced exploitation, similar to mapping out the security measures of a heavily fortified fortress.

In this context, advanced exploitation techniques target network devices, servers, and infrastructure components to identify vulnerabilities that can be exploited to compromise the entire network.

Wireless and IoT vulnerabilities are like hidden backdoors in an otherwise secure building, as they often go unnoticed until an attacker discovers and exploits them.

Advanced exploitation in the wireless and IoT domains involves leveraging weaknesses in wireless protocols, device firmware, and communication channels to gain unauthorized access or control.

Reverse engineering and malware analysis are like deciphering a rival spy's encrypted messages, as they involve dissecting malicious software to understand its functionality and uncover potential vulnerabilities.

Evasive techniques, similar to a skilled spy escaping pursuit, are essential in advanced exploitation to avoid detection by security monitoring and intrusion detection systems.

These techniques include manipulating attack payloads and behaviors to evade security measures.

Engaging with bug bounty programs strategically is akin to a tactical mission in which ethical hackers collaborate with organizations to identify and responsibly disclose vulnerabilities.

Strategic engagement includes careful planning, thorough testing, and effective communication with program operators.

Legal and ethical considerations are paramount in advanced exploitation, much like the adherence to rules of engagement and international law in military operations.

Ethical hackers must ensure that their actions are within the boundaries of the law and adhere to responsible disclosure practices.

The use of advanced exploitation tools and frameworks is like equipping a special forces team with state-of-the-art weaponry, providing hackers with the capabilities needed to carry out complex attacks.

These tools often include exploit development platforms, post-exploitation frameworks, and network reconnaissance tools.

Advanced exploitation methods require continuous learning and research, similar to the ongoing training and intelligence gathering that intelligence agencies undertake.

Hackers must stay updated on the latest attack techniques, vulnerabilities, and defensive strategies to maintain their effectiveness.

Building a legacy as an elite ethical hacker involves not only achieving technical prowess but also mentoring and inspiring the next generation of cybersecurity professionals.

Establishing a reputation for ethical and responsible hacking can contribute to the overall improvement of cybersecurity practices.

In summary, advanced exploitation methods are the pinnacle of offensive cybersecurity, enabling attackers to target complex vulnerabilities, evade detection, and achieve their objectives with precision and sophistication. Much like elite operatives in the world of espionage, ethical hackers who master advanced exploitation techniques possess the skills and knowledge needed to navigate the intricate and dynamic landscape of cybersecurity. By continuously advancing their expertise, maintaining ethical standards, and contributing to the security community, these individuals can make a lasting impact on the field of cybersecurity.

Exploiting zero-day vulnerabilities is a highly advanced and controversial aspect of cybersecurity, akin to wielding a double-edged sword with immense power and responsibility.

Zero-days are security flaws in software or hardware that are unknown to the vendor and, therefore, unpatched, making them prized targets for attackers.

The term "zero-day" refers to the fact that there are zero days of protection for users once a vulnerability is discovered and exploited.

This means that attackers can leverage these vulnerabilities without fear of immediate detection or remediation.

The allure of zero-day vulnerabilities lies in their potency, much like a secret weapon that can bypass all defenses and grant attackers unfettered access.

Zero-days are often used in targeted attacks, espionage campaigns, and cybercriminal activities, making them a matter of grave concern for both individuals and organizations.

The process of exploiting a zero-day vulnerability begins with the discovery or acquisition of the vulnerability itself.

This can occur through various means, such as independent security research, monitoring of underground forums, or even purchasing vulnerabilities on the dark web.

Once a zero-day vulnerability is in the hands of an attacker, it becomes a valuable asset, akin to a hidden treasure chest waiting to be unlocked.

The next step in exploiting a zero-day vulnerability is crafting an exploit, which is like fashioning a key that can open a specific lock.

Exploits are software programs or scripts that take advantage of the vulnerability to gain unauthorized access, execute malicious code, or perform other malicious actions on a target system.

Crafting an exploit for a zero-day vulnerability requires a deep understanding of the vulnerability itself, the target system, and the relevant software components.

It involves meticulous reverse engineering, code analysis, and often the development of custom payloads or shellcode.

Once an exploit is created, it can be deployed in various attack scenarios, much like deploying a covert operative on a mission.

Attackers may use the exploit to gain initial access to a target system, escalate privileges, establish persistence, or achieve other malicious objectives.

The success of an exploit hinges on its ability to evade detection, similar to a skilled infiltrator moving silently through a heavily guarded facility.

To achieve this, attackers may employ evasion techniques, such as polymorphic code, encryption, or obfuscation, to hide the exploit from security monitoring and intrusion detection systems.

Exploiting zero-day vulnerabilities often involves chaining multiple vulnerabilities and techniques together, much like solving a complex puzzle.

Attackers may combine a zero-day exploit with privilege escalation, lateral movement, and post-exploitation activities to achieve their goals.

The potential consequences of zero-day exploits can be catastrophic, much like a devastating weapon of mass destruction.

Attackers can use zero-days to steal sensitive data, disrupt critical infrastructure, sabotage systems, or conduct espionage on a massive scale.

Defenders, on the other hand, face significant challenges in protecting against zero-day exploits.

Since these vulnerabilities are unknown to vendors, there are no patches or official fixes available.

This leaves organizations vulnerable until the vendor becomes aware of the issue, develops a patch, and distributes it to users.

In the meantime, defenders must rely on proactive security measures, such as intrusion detection, network monitoring, and behavioral analysis, to detect and mitigate zero-day attacks.

Additionally, organizations should follow security best practices, including regular software updates, vulnerability scanning, and security awareness training, to reduce the attack surface and minimize the impact of zero-day exploits.

The responsible disclosure of zero-day vulnerabilities is a contentious topic in the cybersecurity community, akin to deciding whether to share sensitive information with the authorities.

Security researchers and ethical hackers often wrestle with the ethical dilemma of when and how to disclose a zero-day vulnerability.

On one hand, responsible disclosure involves notifying the vendor or relevant authorities about the vulnerability to facilitate a patch or mitigation.

This approach aims to protect users and the broader digital ecosystem from potential harm.

On the other hand, some researchers may choose to sell zero-day vulnerabilities to government agencies, cybersecurity firms, or the highest bidder on the black market.

This can be lucrative but raises ethical and legal concerns, as it may contribute to the proliferation of cyber threats.

The decision to disclose or sell a zero-day vulnerability often depends on individual motivations, ethical principles, and legal considerations.

In recent years, bug bounty programs and vulnerability disclosure platforms have provided a more structured and responsible avenue for reporting and addressing zero-day vulnerabilities.

These programs offer financial rewards and recognition to researchers who discover and responsibly disclose security flaws, promoting transparency and collaboration in the cybersecurity community.

In summary, exploiting zero-day vulnerabilities represents a complex and high-stakes aspect of cybersecurity. Much like wielding a double-edged sword, the power to exploit these vulnerabilities comes with immense responsibility. Defenders must remain vigilant, proactive, and prepared to respond to zero-day attacks, while ethical considerations and responsible disclosure practices play a crucial role in mitigating the risks associated with these potent weapons in the digital age.

Chapter 5: Privilege Escalation and Post-Exploitation

Escalating privileges in Windows is a critical aspect of cybersecurity, much like unlocking higher levels of access in a secure facility.

Privilege escalation refers to the process of obtaining higher levels of permissions or privileges on a computer or network than originally granted to a user.

This is a common objective for attackers because it allows them to gain more control over a system and potentially carry out malicious activities with greater impact.

In Windows, user privileges are typically assigned based on the principle of least privilege, which means users are given only the minimum level of access required to perform their tasks.

However, when attackers manage to escalate their privileges, they can break out of these restricted roles and gain control over critical system components.

Privilege escalation attacks can take advantage of various vulnerabilities and misconfigurations, much like finding a weak point in a fortress's defenses.

One common avenue for privilege escalation in Windows is through the exploitation of software vulnerabilities.

Attackers often look for security flaws in Windows itself or in third-party software running on the system.

These vulnerabilities can be exploited to execute arbitrary code with elevated privileges, effectively granting the attacker administrator-level access.

Another technique for privilege escalation is the abuse of misconfigured or vulnerable Windows services and scheduled tasks.

By taking advantage of insecure configurations, attackers can manipulate services or tasks to run malicious code under the context of a privileged user account.

Kernel-level privilege escalation attacks, akin to reaching the heart of a secure fortress, involve exploiting vulnerabilities in the Windows kernel itself.

These attacks are particularly dangerous because they provide attackers with the highest level of access and control over the operating system.

Attackers can use various tools and techniques to escalate privileges in Windows, similar to a skilled locksmith using specialized tools to open a secure lock.

One common tool for privilege escalation is the Metasploit Framework, which includes a wide range of exploits and payloads for Windows.

Metasploit allows attackers to automate the exploitation process and gain elevated privileges quickly.

PowerShell is another powerful tool for privilege escalation in Windows, much like a Swiss Army knife with a multitude of functions.

Attackers can use PowerShell scripts to exploit vulnerabilities, manipulate system configurations, and execute arbitrary code with elevated privileges.

The use of Windows Management Instrumentation (WMI) is another technique for privilege escalation, akin to using a master key to access various parts of a building.

WMI provides a powerful interface for managing Windows systems, and attackers can abuse it to execute commands with higher privileges.

Privilege escalation often involves manipulating access control lists (ACLs) and permissions, similar to tampering with security mechanisms in a secure facility.

By modifying ACLs, attackers can grant themselves additional privileges or take ownership of critical system resources.

Pass-the-hash attacks are a type of privilege escalation that involves stealing hashed credentials from memory and using them to authenticate as a privileged user.

This technique allows attackers to gain access without needing to crack the actual password.

In some cases, privilege escalation attacks rely on a principle called "token impersonation," much like assuming a disguise to gain access to restricted areas.

Attackers can use stolen or forged tokens to impersonate privileged users and perform actions with their level of access.

Privilege escalation can also involve the abuse of user accounts with excessive privileges, similar to infiltrating a secure facility by posing as a trusted employee.

Attackers may target user accounts that have unnecessary administrative privileges and use them to carry out malicious activities.

Detecting and mitigating privilege escalation attacks in Windows requires a multi-layered security approach, much like fortifying a well-defended fortress.

Regularly applying security updates and patches is essential to address known vulnerabilities that attackers may exploit.

Implementing robust access controls, like the use of least privilege principles, can limit the impact of privilege escalation attacks.

Monitoring system logs and auditing user activities is crucial for detecting suspicious behavior and privilege escalation attempts.

Intrusion detection systems (IDS) and security information and event management (SIEM) solutions can help organizations identify and respond to privilege escalation incidents.

Implementing application whitelisting and strong authentication mechanisms can also prevent attackers from gaining unauthorized access.

Educating users about security best practices and the risks of privilege escalation attacks is vital to create a security-conscious culture.

In summary, privilege escalation in Windows is a significant concern in cybersecurity, as it can lead to the compromise of critical systems and data. Much like infiltrating a secure facility, attackers employ various techniques and tools to escalate their privileges. Organizations must adopt proactive security measures, such as patch management, access control, monitoring, and user education, to defend against privilege escalation attacks effectively. By understanding the tactics employed by attackers, defenders can better safeguard their Windows environments and protect against unauthorized access and data breaches.

Post-exploitation frameworks are powerful tools in the arsenal of cybersecurity professionals, akin to the specialized equipment used by investigators to gather crucial evidence after a breach.

These frameworks are designed to help ethical hackers, penetration testers, and red teamers maintain control over compromised systems, gather intelligence, and achieve their objectives during the post-exploitation phase of an attack.

Post-exploitation refers to the activities carried out by an attacker after they have successfully infiltrated a target system, much like a skilled operative navigating an enemy stronghold.

These activities include maintaining access, privilege escalation, lateral movement, data exfiltration, and covering tracks to avoid detection.

Post-exploitation frameworks provide a structured and efficient way to carry out these tasks, offering a range of capabilities and modules that facilitate the attacker's goals.

One well-known post-exploitation framework is Metasploit, which is widely used by cybersecurity professionals and attackers alike.

Metasploit allows users to exploit vulnerabilities, gain access to systems, and then utilize post-exploitation modules to maintain control, collect information, and execute various actions on compromised hosts.

Another popular post-exploitation framework is PowerShell Empire, which leverages the capabilities of PowerShell, a legitimate Windows scripting language, to conduct post-exploitation activities.

PowerShell Empire provides a wide range of modules for tasks such as privilege escalation, credential theft, lateral movement, and data exfiltration.

Cobalt Strike is a commercial post-exploitation framework that is particularly popular among penetration testers and red teamers.

It offers a comprehensive set of tools for maintaining access, conducting reconnaissance, and launching advanced attacks on compromised systems.

Many post-exploitation frameworks support multiple operating systems, allowing attackers to maintain control over a diverse range of targets, much like a master key that can unlock various doors.

This flexibility is essential for attackers who need to navigate heterogeneous environments.

Post-exploitation frameworks often include modules for privilege escalation, which is the process of gaining higher-level access or permissions on a compromised system.

Privilege escalation is crucial for attackers because it allows them to perform more actions and access sensitive resources.

These modules may exploit known vulnerabilities, abuse misconfigurations, or leverage weaknesses in the target system to elevate privileges.

Lateral movement is another critical aspect of post-exploitation, akin to a spy moving stealthily through an enemy compound.

Attackers use lateral movement techniques to pivot from one compromised system to another within a network, spreading their influence and gaining access to additional resources.

Post-exploitation frameworks offer modules that enable lateral movement, often relying on stolen credentials, pass-the-hash attacks, or other techniques to move laterally.

Data exfiltration is a common objective during post-exploitation, much like a spy extracting valuable information.

Attackers use post-exploitation frameworks to steal sensitive data from compromised systems and transmit it to external servers or storage locations.

These frameworks provide modules for file transfers, remote data access, and data compression to facilitate the exfiltration process.

Maintaining persistence is crucial for attackers in the post-exploitation phase, similar to ensuring a foothold in enemy territory.

Post-exploitation frameworks offer mechanisms to establish persistence on compromised systems, allowing attackers to maintain access even after a system is rebooted or security measures are applied.

Persistence techniques may involve creating scheduled tasks, modifying system configurations, or injecting malicious code into legitimate processes.

Covering tracks is an essential aspect of post-exploitation, akin to erasing evidence of an infiltration.

Attackers use post-exploitation frameworks to remove logs, delete artifacts, and cover their digital footprints to avoid detection by system administrators and security teams.

These frameworks may provide modules for clearing event logs, removing forensic artifacts, and sanitizing the compromised system.

Post-exploitation frameworks often include features for command and control (C2), similar to a communications channel between an operative and their handler.

These C2 channels allow attackers to issue commands, receive responses, and interact with compromised systems remotely.

Communication may occur over various protocols, such as HTTP, HTTPS, DNS, or custom channels, to avoid detection.

Advanced post-exploitation frameworks offer scripting capabilities, allowing users to develop custom modules and automate specific post-exploitation tasks, similar to creating specialized tools for specific operations.

Custom scripting enhances the flexibility and adaptability of these frameworks to meet the unique requirements of different engagements.

Ethical considerations are paramount when using post-exploitation frameworks, akin to adhering to a code of conduct in an intelligence operation.

Ethical hackers, penetration testers, and red teamers must use these tools responsibly, within the boundaries of their engagement scope, and in compliance with relevant laws and regulations.

In summary, post-exploitation frameworks are indispensable tools for cybersecurity professionals tasked with maintaining control over compromised systems, gathering intelligence, and achieving their objectives during the post-exploitation phase of an engagement. Much like the specialized equipment used by investigators, these frameworks provide a structured and efficient way to carry out a wide range of post-exploitation activities. However, their use must always be guided by ethical considerations and legal compliance to ensure responsible and ethical cybersecurity practices.

Chapter 6: Web Application Security Assessment

SQL injection is a prevalent and dangerous type of cyber attack that targets the security vulnerabilities in database-driven web applications, much like a cunning infiltrator exploiting weaknesses in a fortress's defenses.

This attack technique allows malicious actors to manipulate the input fields of a web application, injecting SQL queries into them, and potentially gaining unauthorized access to the database.

The consequences of successful SQL injection attacks can be severe, akin to an infiltrator accessing a treasure trove of sensitive information.

Attackers can steal, modify, or delete data, execute administrative operations, and potentially compromise the security of an entire system.

SQL injection attacks are not limited to any specific type of database management system or web application framework.

They can affect a wide range of platforms, making them a pervasive threat in the realm of web security.

The core concept behind SQL injection is exploiting improper input validation, much like a spy taking advantage of a guard's momentary lapse in attention.

Web applications often accept user input, such as search queries, login credentials, or form data, and pass that input to a database without adequate validation or sanitization.

Attackers capitalize on this weakness by injecting malicious SQL code into these input fields.

The injected SQL code becomes part of the query executed by the database, allowing attackers to manipulate its behavior.

SQL injection attacks come in various forms, much like a spy employing different tactics to infiltrate a target.

One common type is "classic" SQL injection, where attackers inject SQL statements directly into input fields.

For example, an attacker might input " ' OR 1=1 --" into a login field, tricking the application into treating the input as part of a legitimate SQL query and granting unauthorized access.

Blind SQL injection is another variant, where attackers exploit vulnerabilities without directly observing the application's responses.

Instead, they use Boolean-based or time-based techniques to infer information indirectly.

For instance, an attacker might use payloads that cause the application to delay its response if a specific condition is met.

Time delays can be used to confirm the presence of certain data or conditions in the database.

Out-of-band SQL injection involves attackers exfiltrating data using an alternate communication channel, such as DNS requests or HTTP requests to a controlled server.

This technique is useful when direct retrieval of data from the application's response is not possible.

Second-order SQL injection occurs when an application stores user input that includes malicious SQL code in a database.

The injected code only executes when the input is later retrieved and processed by the application.

Blind SQL injection attacks can be particularly challenging to detect and mitigate, as they do not produce immediate, visible results.

Protection against SQL injection begins with secure coding practices, akin to fortifying a fortress's defenses against infiltration.

Developers must validate and sanitize all user inputs to ensure they cannot be used to inject malicious SQL code.

Parameterized queries and prepared statements are effective techniques to prevent SQL injection, as they separate user input from SQL code.

Web application firewalls (WAFs) are another layer of defense, much like guards stationed at various checkpoints within a fortress.

WAFs inspect incoming traffic and can block known SQL injection patterns, but they are not foolproof and should be used in conjunction with secure coding practices.

Security testing and code reviews are crucial for identifying and addressing SQL injection vulnerabilities during the development phase, much like thorough inspections of a fortress's defenses.

Regular vulnerability scanning and penetration testing can help organizations discover and remediate SQL injection vulnerabilities in existing applications.

Database security measures, such as using the principle of least privilege, limiting direct database access, and monitoring for suspicious activity, can mitigate the impact of SQL injection attacks.

Intrusion detection systems (IDS) and security information and event management (SIEM) solutions can help detect and respond to SQL injection attempts, similar to alerting guards to unusual activity.

Beyond SQL injection, web applications face a broader array of injection attacks, much like various tactics used by infiltrators in espionage.

These attacks target different application components and data formats, including:

Command injection: Attackers inject malicious commands into application inputs that are subsequently executed by the operating system.

XML injection: Attackers manipulate XML input to exploit vulnerabilities in XML parsers, potentially causing data leaks or service disruptions.

LDAP injection: Attackers inject malicious LDAP queries into application inputs, potentially gaining unauthorized access to directory services.

XPath injection: Attackers manipulate XPath queries in XML-based applications, similar to SQL injection, to extract data or bypass authentication.

NoSQL injection: Attackers exploit vulnerabilities in NoSQL databases by injecting malicious input, potentially gaining unauthorized access or causing data leakage.

Protecting against injection attacks beyond SQL injection requires a holistic approach to application security, much like securing all entry points in a fortress.

Developers must validate and sanitize inputs, implement strong access controls, and follow secure coding practices for all application components.

Security testing and code reviews should encompass a broader range of injection attack vectors, and organizations should consider using web application firewalls and intrusion detection systems to detect and block such attacks.

In summary, SQL injection is a prevalent and dangerous attack that targets vulnerabilities in web applications' input validation. Much like infiltrators exploiting weaknesses in a fortress's defenses, attackers manipulate user inputs to inject malicious SQL code into database queries. Protecting against SQL injection and related injection attacks requires secure coding practices, input validation, security testing, and the use of security tools like web application firewalls and intrusion detection systems. By addressing these vulnerabilities, organizations can strengthen their web application security and reduce the risk of data breaches and other security incidents.

Chapter 7: Network Security and Infrastructure Testing

Assessing network architecture is a critical aspect of cybersecurity, much like evaluating the structural integrity of a building before occupancy.

A network is the backbone of any modern organization's IT infrastructure, providing the connectivity and communication channels necessary for business operations.

Network architecture encompasses the design, layout, components, and protocols that govern how data flows within an organization's network.

Conducting a comprehensive assessment of network architecture is essential for identifying vulnerabilities, weaknesses, and areas for improvement.

This assessment involves a thorough examination of the network's physical and logical components, akin to inspecting the infrastructure of a building for potential issues.

Physical components include hardware devices such as routers, switches, firewalls, servers, and network cables.

These components form the tangible foundation of the network and must be properly configured, secured, and maintained.

Logical components, on the other hand, encompass network protocols, configurations, access controls, and traffic patterns.

They define the rules and operations that govern data transmission and access within the network.

A network architecture assessment begins with an inventory of all physical devices and their configurations, much like documenting the structure and materials of a building.

This inventory helps identify outdated or unsupported hardware, misconfigurations, and potential points of failure.

Reviewing network diagrams and documentation is crucial for understanding the network's layout, similar to studying blueprints and plans for a building.

These diagrams provide insights into how devices are connected, the flow of data, and the overall structure of the network.

Mapping network segments and zones is essential to assess how different parts of the network are isolated and secured, much like delineating different sections within a building.

Segmentation helps contain potential security breaches and limit the lateral movement of attackers.

Assessing network traffic patterns and flows provides insights into data transfer volumes, anomalies, and potential bottlenecks, akin to evaluating the movement of people and materials within a building.

Monitoring and analyzing traffic can reveal suspicious activities and help optimize network performance.

Security assessments of network architecture are paramount, similar to conducting security checks on building entrances and exits.

This involves reviewing firewall configurations, access control lists, intrusion detection and prevention systems, and encryption mechanisms.

Evaluating the effectiveness of security controls ensures that the network is adequately protected against external threats.

Assessing user access controls and authentication mechanisms is crucial to ensure that only authorized individuals have access to network resources, much like controlling who has keys to the building.

This assessment includes reviewing user account policies, password policies, and multi-factor authentication implementations.

Network segmentation and isolation are vital for containing security breaches, similar to compartmentalizing different sections of a building.

Evaluating the effectiveness of segmentation controls helps prevent lateral movement by attackers.

Vulnerability scanning and penetration testing are valuable tools in assessing network architecture's security posture, akin to conducting structural integrity tests on a building.

These tests identify vulnerabilities, misconfigurations, and potential entry points for attackers.

Traffic analysis tools and network monitoring solutions can help detect and investigate suspicious activities, much like security cameras and surveillance systems in a building.

These tools provide visibility into network traffic and enable security teams to respond to incidents promptly.

Assessing network architecture for compliance with industry standards and regulations is essential to ensure legal and regulatory requirements are met, similar to obtaining permits and certifications for building occupancy.

Compliance assessments involve aligning network configurations and policies with specific requirements, such as the Payment Card Industry Data Security Standard

(PCI DSS) or the Health Insurance Portability and Accountability Act (HIPAA).

Evaluating disaster recovery and business continuity plans is vital for network resilience, akin to having evacuation and emergency response plans for a building.

These plans outline procedures for data backup, recovery, and continuity of operations in the event of network failures or disasters.

Scalability and performance assessments are necessary to ensure the network can meet the organization's growing demands, much like evaluating the capacity of a building to accommodate increasing occupancy.

Assessments may involve load testing, capacity planning, and optimizing network resources.

Documentation and knowledge transfer are crucial components of a network architecture assessment, similar to providing building occupants with manuals and emergency procedures.

Ensuring that network configurations, diagrams, and procedures are well-documented enables efficient management and troubleshooting.

As technology evolves, it is essential to assess the network's readiness for emerging technologies, similar to upgrading building infrastructure to accommodate new amenities.

Evaluating the network's adaptability to cloud computing, Internet of Things (IoT) devices, and other innovations is critical for future-proofing the architecture.

Budgetary considerations play a role in assessing network architecture, much like budget constraints impact building maintenance and upgrades.

The assessment should prioritize recommendations based on available resources and the organization's strategic objectives.

Risk assessment and threat modeling are fundamental aspects of network architecture assessment, akin to evaluating security risks and vulnerabilities in a building's design.

Identifying potential threats and their impacts helps prioritize security measures.

In summary, assessing network architecture is a multifaceted process that involves evaluating physical and logical components, security measures, compliance, scalability, and readiness for emerging technologies. Similar to assessing a building's structural integrity and safety measures, a thorough network architecture assessment is essential for maintaining a secure, efficient, and resilient IT infrastructure. Organizations must regularly review and update their network architecture to adapt to evolving technology landscapes and address emerging security threats. Hardening network defenses is a critical aspect of cybersecurity, much like reinforcing the walls and fortifications of a castle to withstand external threats. In the digital age, networks are under constant siege from cybercriminals, making it imperative to strengthen their security measures.

Network hardening involves a series of proactive measures designed to minimize vulnerabilities and enhance the resilience of an organization's IT infrastructure. These measures encompass both technical configurations and security policies, similar to establishing rules and safeguards within a castle.

The objective of network hardening is to reduce the attack surface, making it more challenging for attackers to exploit weaknesses and gain unauthorized access.

One fundamental aspect of network hardening is patch management, akin to repairing and maintaining the physical structures of a castle. Regularly applying security patches and updates to operating systems, applications, and firmware is essential for addressing known vulnerabilities. Outdated software can serve as a gateway for attackers, much like a deteriorating wall that provides an entry point for intruders.

Network segmentation is another critical component of hardening network defenses, similar to dividing a castle into different sections with controlled access.

By segmenting the network into isolated zones, organizations can limit the lateral movement of attackers, contain breaches, and protect sensitive data.

Implementing strong access controls is vital for restricting user privileges and limiting exposure to potential threats, akin to allowing only authorized individuals to enter specific areas of a castle.

Access controls involve user authentication, authorization, and multi-factor authentication to ensure that only authorized users can access network resources.

Firewalls are essential tools in network hardening, much like defensive fortifications that repel attackers.

Firewalls filter incoming and outgoing network traffic, blocking malicious traffic and enforcing security policies.

Intrusion detection and prevention systems (IDPS) play a crucial role in network hardening by monitoring for suspicious activity and alerting security teams to potential threats, similar to sentries stationed on castle walls.

IDPS can detect and block attacks in real-time, helping organizations respond swiftly to security incidents.

Implementing encryption is essential for protecting data in transit and at rest, akin to safeguarding valuable treasures within a castle.

Using encryption protocols such as HTTPS, SSL/TLS, and VPNs ensures that sensitive information remains confidential and secure.

Hardening network devices, such as routers, switches, and access points, is vital for preventing unauthorized access and configurations, much like securing the gates and entrances of a castle.

Default passwords and unnecessary services should be disabled, and strong authentication methods should be enforced.

Regularly auditing and monitoring network configurations help identify and rectify security weaknesses, similar to conducting routine inspections of a castle's defenses.

Network administrators should review configurations, access logs, and security policies to ensure they align with best practices.

Implementing security information and event management (SIEM) systems can help organizations centralize and analyze security-related data, akin to having a command center to monitor castle defenses.

SIEM solutions provide real-time visibility into network activity, enabling security teams to detect and respond to threats effectively.

Hardening the human element of network defenses is crucial, similar to training and arming the soldiers defending a castle.

Security awareness training educates employees about cybersecurity best practices, threats, and social engineering tactics.

Regularly updating and testing incident response plans is essential for ensuring that organizations can effectively respond to security incidents, akin to having a well-defined emergency response plan in a castle.

These plans outline procedures for identifying, containing, mitigating, and recovering from security breaches.

Implementing endpoint security solutions, such as antivirus software and endpoint detection and response (EDR) tools, is vital for protecting individual devices on the network, much like equipping soldiers with armor and weapons.

Endpoint security solutions can detect and prevent malware infections and other threats.

Conducting regular vulnerability assessments and penetration testing helps organizations identify and address weaknesses in their network defenses, similar to hiring skilled archers to test the castle's defenses.

Vulnerability assessments scan the network for known vulnerabilities, while penetration testing simulates real-world attacks to uncover potential risks.

Implementing network security policies and procedures is essential for ensuring that security measures are consistently applied, akin to having a set of rules and guidelines for castle defense.

These policies should address password management, data classification, incident response, and other security-related aspects.

Monitoring and logging network activity provide organizations with a valuable source of information for detecting and investigating security incidents, similar to keeping a record of castle activities.

Logs can reveal suspicious behavior, unauthorized access attempts, and other indicators of compromise.

Regularly backing up critical data and systems is crucial for ensuring business continuity and data recovery in the event of a security incident, much like safeguarding important documents and treasures within a castle.

Backup and recovery plans should be tested regularly to verify their effectiveness.

Network hardening is an ongoing process that requires continuous monitoring, assessment, and adaptation to evolving threats, similar to maintaining and upgrading castle defenses to withstand changing siege tactics.

Regular security audits and risk assessments help organizations stay proactive in identifying and addressing vulnerabilities.

In summary, hardening network defenses is essential for safeguarding an organization's IT infrastructure in an increasingly hostile digital landscape. Similar to fortifying the walls and defenses of a castle, network hardening measures involve patch management, network segmentation, access controls, firewalls, intrusion detection systems, encryption, and endpoint security. Moreover, the human element plays a vital role in network security through security awareness training and incident response planning. To effectively defend against cyber threats, organizations must embrace a comprehensive and proactive approach to network hardening, continually adapting to emerging challenges and threats.

Chapter 8: Wireless and IoT Vulnerabilities

Cracking Wi-Fi encryption is a subject that raises both curiosity and concern in the world of cybersecurity, much like deciphering an intricate code or puzzle.

Wi-Fi networks are ubiquitous in our digital lives, providing wireless connectivity for a multitude of devices.

To secure these networks and protect sensitive data, Wi-Fi encryption is employed, serving as a digital lock on the door to the network.

Encryption algorithms, such as WEP (Wired Equivalent Privacy), WPA (Wi-Fi Protected Access), and WPA2/WPA3, are used to encode data transmitted between devices and the Wi-Fi access point.

The objective of Wi-Fi encryption is to prevent unauthorized access to network traffic and maintain the confidentiality of data, much like safeguarding secret messages from prying eyes.

However, the concept of Wi-Fi encryption being "unbreakable" or "foolproof" is a misconception.

While modern encryption standards like WPA2 and WPA3 are robust and significantly more secure than their predecessors, they are not entirely immune to attack.

Cracking Wi-Fi encryption involves attempting to discover the network's pre-shared key (PSK) or passphrase, which is used to encrypt and decrypt data.

Attackers employ various techniques and tools to bypass this security measure, similar to trying to pick a lock.

One common method used in cracking Wi-Fi encryption is the brute-force attack, where an attacker attempts all possible combinations of characters to guess the PSK.

This approach is time-consuming and computationally intensive, as it requires testing a vast number of combinations, similar to trying every possible key to open a lock.

To speed up the process, attackers often use precomputed lists of potential keys, known as "rainbow tables," or employ powerful hardware to perform the calculations more quickly.

Dictionary attacks are another method attackers use to crack Wi-Fi encryption, much like trying common words and phrases as keys.

Attackers leverage dictionaries of commonly used words, phrases, and passwords to guess the PSK.

These dictionaries can be extensive and include various languages and combinations.

As a defense against dictionary attacks, users are advised to choose strong and unique passphrases.

Wi-Fi encryption cracking techniques also include the use of software tools that automate the process, similar to using lock-picking kits.

Tools like Aircrack-ng and Hashcat are designed for testing Wi-Fi network security and can accelerate the cracking process.

While these techniques may sound concerning, it's important to note that strong, complex passphrases significantly increase the time and effort required for successful cracking, similar to a more intricate lock requiring more skill and time to pick.

Using a combination of upper and lower-case letters, numbers, and special characters in a passphrase can make it exponentially harder to crack.

Moreover, modern Wi-Fi encryption standards, such as WPA3, incorporate security features like Simultaneous Authentication of Equals (SAE), which further strengthen protection against offline attacks.

Another consideration in cracking Wi-Fi encryption is the security protocol used by the network.

WEP, for instance, is notoriously vulnerable to cracking, as it relies on weak encryption algorithms.

WPA2, while more secure, can still be susceptible to attacks if a weak passphrase is used.

WPA3, on the other hand, introduces more robust encryption and better protection against brute-force and dictionary attacks, making it the preferred choice for securing Wi-Fi networks.

To defend against Wi-Fi encryption cracking, users should follow best practices for Wi-Fi security, much like fortifying the defenses of a fortress.

This includes using strong passphrases, enabling WPA3 if supported, regularly updating Wi-Fi equipment firmware, and employing additional security measures like MAC address filtering and intrusion detection systems.

Network administrators should also monitor for suspicious activity and implement proper network segmentation to limit potential exposure.

Moreover, Wi-Fi encryption cracking attempts often involve unauthorized access to networks, which is illegal and unethical.

Engaging in such activities can lead to severe legal consequences, much like attempting to break into a secure facility.

In summary, cracking Wi-Fi encryption is a complex process that involves various techniques, tools, and vulnerabilities.

While modern encryption standards like WPA3 offer robust protection, they are not invulnerable to determined attackers.

Users and network administrators should follow best practices for Wi-Fi security to minimize the risk of unauthorized access and protect sensitive data.

Remember that attempting to crack Wi-Fi encryption is illegal and unethical, and engaging in such activities can result in serious consequences.

IoT device exploitation is a topic of growing concern in the realm of cybersecurity, much like uncovering hidden vulnerabilities in a complex system.

The Internet of Things (IoT) has revolutionized our daily lives, bringing convenience and automation through interconnected devices.

However, this interconnectedness also introduces new avenues for cyberattacks, making IoT device security a paramount issue.

Exploiting IoT devices involves identifying weaknesses, vulnerabilities, and misconfigurations that could be leveraged by malicious actors, similar to finding weaknesses in a fortress's defenses.

IoT devices encompass a wide range of technologies, including smart thermostats, cameras, doorbells, refrigerators, and industrial sensors, much like diverse components within a complex system.

These devices connect to the internet or local networks, often collecting and transmitting sensitive data.

One of the primary challenges in IoT device exploitation is the sheer diversity of devices, each with its own firmware, hardware, and software stack, akin to deciphering different languages within a complex system.

These devices may run on embedded operating systems and employ various communication protocols, making them a complex ecosystem to assess.

Exploiting IoT devices can have severe consequences, similar to compromising a critical component of a complex system.

Attackers can gain unauthorized access, steal sensitive information, disrupt device functionality, or even use compromised devices to launch attacks on other systems.

To exploit IoT devices, attackers typically begin by identifying potential targets, similar to identifying weak points in a complex system.

They may scan the internet or local networks for devices with known vulnerabilities or misconfigurations.

Common attack vectors include weak default credentials, unpatched software, and insecure communication protocols.

Once a vulnerable device is identified, attackers may attempt to gain unauthorized access, much like infiltrating a secured area within a complex system.

This can involve exploiting known vulnerabilities or using techniques like password cracking or credential stuffing.

IoT devices often lack robust security measures, such as proper authentication and authorization mechanisms, similar to inadequate access controls within a complex system.

As a result, attackers may find it easier to gain access.

Once inside, attackers can carry out various malicious activities, such as eavesdropping on communications, manipulating device functionality, or exfiltrating sensitive data, much like manipulating key components in a complex system.

Furthermore, attackers may use compromised IoT devices as part of botnets, similar to controlling multiple elements within a complex system.

These botnets can be employed in distributed denial-of-service (DDoS) attacks, spreading malware, or carrying out other malicious actions.

IoT device manufacturers often face challenges in maintaining device security, similar to ensuring the reliability of components within a complex system.

Firmware updates and security patches may not be consistently provided or applied by device owners, leaving devices vulnerable to known exploits.

Moreover, the lifespan of IoT devices can vary significantly, and older devices may not receive updates, increasing their susceptibility to exploitation.

To defend against IoT device exploitation, device manufacturers and owners must prioritize security, much like fortifying the defenses of a complex system.

This includes implementing strong authentication and authorization mechanisms, conducting regular security assessments, and promptly addressing vulnerabilities and misconfigurations.

Device owners should change default credentials, keep firmware and software up to date, and segment IoT devices from critical networks when possible.

Network monitoring and intrusion detection systems can help identify suspicious activity and potential IoT device compromises, similar to surveillance and security measures within a complex system.

Additionally, regulatory bodies and industry standards play a vital role in establishing security requirements and guidelines for IoT devices, akin to establishing safety and compliance standards within complex systems.

Ensuring that IoT devices adhere to these standards can contribute to overall security.

In summary, IoT device exploitation is a pressing cybersecurity concern, as the proliferation of interconnected devices creates new attack surfaces and vulnerabilities.

Attacks on IoT devices can lead to data breaches, privacy violations, and disruptions in critical systems, much like compromising key components within a complex system.

To mitigate the risks associated with IoT device exploitation, manufacturers, device owners, and regulatory bodies must collaborate to establish robust security measures and guidelines.

Ultimately, the security of IoT devices is essential to ensuring the continued benefits and convenience of the Internet of Things while safeguarding against potential threats.

Chapter 9: Penetration Testing and Red Teaming

Engaging in red team operations is a practice in cybersecurity that simulates real-world attacks to test an organization's defenses, much like staging a mock battle to assess a fortress's readiness.

Red teaming is a proactive and adversarial approach aimed at identifying vulnerabilities and weaknesses within an organization's security posture.

The term "red team" is derived from military exercises where one team, the "red team," assumes the role of the adversary to challenge the other team's defenses, similar to an opposing force attempting to breach a fortress.

In cybersecurity, red team operations involve a team of skilled professionals, often called "red teamers," who emulate the tactics, techniques, and procedures (TTPs) of real-world threat actors, akin to adversaries plotting strategies to infiltrate a fortress.

The goal of red teaming is to provide organizations with a comprehensive assessment of their security posture, uncovering blind spots and weaknesses that may not be apparent through traditional assessments and audits, much like discovering hidden vulnerabilities within a fortress.

Red teamers adopt an offensive mindset, thinking like adversaries to find creative ways to breach an organization's defenses, similar to attackers looking for weak points in a fortress's walls.

Engaging in red team operations typically begins with scoping and planning, where the organization and the red team collaboratively define the objectives and rules of engagement, ensuring alignment with security goals and priorities, much like strategizing for a military exercise.

Red team operations encompass various aspects of an organization's security, including networks, applications, physical security, and even social engineering, similar to considering all aspects of fortress defense.

Red teamers employ a variety of tactics during their assessments, such as penetration testing, vulnerability exploitation, and scenario-based exercises, aiming to simulate real-world attack scenarios, much like adversaries employing diverse tactics to breach fortress defenses.

One crucial aspect of red team operations is the reconnaissance phase, where red teamers gather intelligence and information about the organization, similar to an adversary conducting surveillance of a fortress.

This may involve open-source intelligence (OSINT) gathering, network scanning, and social engineering to identify potential weaknesses.

Once the reconnaissance is complete, red teamers develop attack strategies and tactics tailored to the organization's specific environment, similar to formulating a plan to breach a fortress.

During the assessment phase, red teamers execute their attack scenarios, attempting to bypass security controls and gain unauthorized access to critical assets, much like adversaries attempting to infiltrate fortress walls.

They may exploit vulnerabilities, use malware, or employ social engineering techniques to achieve their objectives.

Throughout the assessment, red teamers continually adapt their tactics and techniques based on the organization's responses, similar to adversaries adjusting their strategies when facing resistance in a fortress.

The objective is to challenge the organization's incident response and detection capabilities.

One important aspect of red team operations is the documentation and reporting phase, where red teamers provide detailed reports of their findings, much like delivering an assessment of fortress vulnerabilities.

These reports outline the weaknesses discovered, the methods used, and recommendations for improving security.

The organization can use these reports to prioritize remediation efforts and enhance its security posture.

Red team operations often culminate in a debriefing session, where the red team and the organization's security team discuss the assessment's outcomes and lessons learned, similar to analyzing the results of a military exercise.

This collaboration fosters knowledge sharing and helps the organization understand its strengths and weaknesses better.

The benefits of engaging in red team operations are numerous, similar to the advantages of thoroughly testing fortress defenses.

First, red teaming provides a realistic assessment of an organization's security posture, helping it identify vulnerabilities that may have otherwise gone unnoticed.

Second, it fosters a proactive approach to security, encouraging organizations to continually improve their defenses based on real-world threats.

Third, red teaming enhances incident response and detection capabilities by challenging security teams to detect and respond to simulated attacks.

Fourth, it helps organizations comply with regulatory requirements and industry best practices by demonstrating due diligence in assessing security controls.

Fifth, red teaming enables organizations to evaluate the effectiveness of security awareness training and employee responses to social engineering attempts, similar to training soldiers to respond effectively to threats in a fortress.

However, red team operations also come with challenges, much like any complex exercise or operation.

One challenge is ensuring that the red team operates ethically and within legal boundaries, similar to adhering to rules of engagement in military exercises.

Ethical considerations are paramount to prevent harm and ensure that assessments do not cross ethical or legal boundaries.

Another challenge is maintaining a balance between the red team's autonomy and the organization's objectives, ensuring that the assessment remains focused on the organization's security goals.

Additionally, red team operations can be resource-intensive, requiring skilled professionals, time, and budget, similar to allocating resources for a military exercise.

Despite these challenges, red team operations are a valuable tool in strengthening an organization's security posture, similar to fortifying a fortress's defenses through rigorous testing.

By adopting an adversarial mindset and simulating real-world threats, organizations can better prepare themselves to defend against evolving cybersecurity risks.

In summary, engaging in red team operations is a proactive and valuable approach to assessing and enhancing an organization's security posture.

Similar to military exercises, red teaming involves skilled professionals emulating real-world threat actors to identify vulnerabilities and weaknesses.

By doing so, organizations can strengthen their defenses, improve incident response capabilities, and better protect their assets in an ever-changing cybersecurity landscape.

Reporting and recommendations play a pivotal role in the cybersecurity landscape, serving as the culmination of assessments, much like presenting findings and solutions after a comprehensive investigation.

Effective reporting is the cornerstone of a cybersecurity professional's role, similar to communicating the results of a complex analysis.

It involves presenting the outcomes of security assessments, whether they are penetration tests, vulnerability assessments, or red team operations, in a clear and actionable manner.

Reports serve as a bridge between the technical findings and the decision-makers within an organization, much like translating intricate technical details into understandable language for key stakeholders.

A well-structured cybersecurity report not only conveys the discovered vulnerabilities and weaknesses but also provides insights into the potential impact of these issues on the organization's security posture, similar to explaining the significance of identified problems.

The first step in creating a meaningful cybersecurity report is to understand the target audience, akin to tailoring the message to the intended recipients.

Different stakeholders have varying levels of technical expertise and responsibilities within the organization, so the report's content and format should align with their needs.

For technical staff, the report may include in-depth technical details, such as the methods used to exploit vulnerabilities and proof-of-concept (PoC) demonstrations, similar to providing detailed evidence in a legal case.

However, for executives and non-technical decision-makers, the report should focus on the broader impact and potential business risks associated with the findings, much like presenting a case's implications to a jury.

A well-structured cybersecurity report typically follows a standardized format, similar to the chapters of a book, which helps ensure consistency and clarity.

The report's structure typically includes an executive summary, an introduction, methodology, findings, risk assessment, recommendations, and a conclusion, similar to organizing the key elements of a persuasive argument.

The executive summary is a concise overview of the assessment's objectives, methodology, and high-level findings, designed to provide a quick understanding of the assessment's outcomes, much like the blurb on the back cover of a book.

The introduction sets the context for the assessment, outlining its purpose and scope, akin to the opening chapters of a book that establish the story's setting and premise.

The methodology section details the approach, tools, and techniques used during the assessment, providing transparency about how the findings were obtained, similar to explaining the research methods used in a study.

The findings section is the heart of the report, presenting the identified vulnerabilities, weaknesses, and areas of concern, much like the central plot and conflicts in a narrative.

Each finding should be clearly described, including its severity, potential impact, and any relevant technical details, similar to providing a thorough description of key events in a story.

Incorporating evidence, such as screenshots or logs, can enhance the credibility of the findings, much like including supporting evidence in an argument.

The risk assessment section evaluates the potential business impact of the findings, considering factors like likelihood, potential harm, and mitigating controls, similar to weighing the consequences of a decision in a story.

This section helps organizations prioritize remediation efforts based on the risks posed by each finding.

The recommendations section provides actionable guidance for addressing the identified vulnerabilities and weaknesses, much like suggesting solutions to the challenges faced by characters in a narrative.

Recommendations should be specific, prioritized, and tailored to the organization's environment, enabling stakeholders to make informed decisions about remediation efforts.

In addition to technical recommendations, it is essential to include practical advice for mitigating the identified risks, such as policy changes, user training, or process improvements, similar to offering guidance on personal growth and development in a self-help book.

The conclusion summarizes the key takeaways from the assessment and reiterates the importance of addressing the identified issues, much like the concluding remarks that leave a lasting impression in a book.

In addition to the formal structure, the tone and language of the report are crucial, similar to maintaining a consistent narrative voice in a book.

Reports should be written in clear, concise language, avoiding technical jargon whenever possible to ensure that all stakeholders can understand the content.

Visual aids, such as charts, graphs, and diagrams, can help illustrate complex concepts and findings, much like using illustrations to enhance a story's narrative.

To make the report even more impactful, it can be beneficial to include a roadmap or action plan that outlines the steps the organization should take to address the identified issues, similar to providing a path forward for characters in a story.

Once the report is complete, it should undergo a thorough review process to ensure accuracy, clarity, and consistency, similar to editing and proofreading a manuscript before publication.

This review should involve not only the author but also subject matter experts and stakeholders who can provide valuable insights and feedback.

Finally, the report should be delivered to the organization's leadership and relevant teams in a timely manner, accompanied by a presentation that highlights the key findings and recommendations, much like an author presenting their book to an audience.

The presentation allows for a more interactive discussion and provides an opportunity to address any questions or concerns raised by the stakeholders.

In summary, reporting and recommendations are essential components of the cybersecurity assessment process, similar to presenting the findings and solutions in a compelling story.

Effective reporting requires tailoring the content and format to the target audience, following a structured approach, and using clear and concise language.

By delivering well-structured and impactful reports, cybersecurity professionals can help organizations make informed decisions to improve their security posture and mitigate potential risks, much like authors conveying meaningful narratives to their readers.

Chapter 10: Bug Hunter's Toolkit: Tools and Tips for Skilled Hunters

In the world of bug hunting, having the right tools at your disposal is akin to having a well-equipped toolbox for various tasks.

These tools are essential for identifying vulnerabilities, testing security controls, and ultimately enhancing the overall security posture of a system or application.

Bug hunters, whether they are security researchers, ethical hackers, or penetration testers, rely on a combination of specialized software and scripts to aid them in their endeavors, much like skilled craftsmen using specific tools for their trade.

These essential bug hunting tools can be categorized into several key areas, each serving a unique purpose in the bug hunting process.

First and foremost, scanners and vulnerability assessment tools play a crucial role in bug hunting, similar to diagnostic instruments in a doctor's toolkit.

These tools are designed to automatically identify known vulnerabilities and misconfigurations in software, web applications, or networks.

For example, web application scanners like Burp Suite and OWASP ZAP are widely used to detect common web application vulnerabilities such as SQL injection, cross-site scripting (XSS), and insecure authentication.

Similarly, network scanners like Nmap help bug hunters map out network topologies and discover open ports and services, akin to a map and compass for navigating uncharted territory.

In addition to scanners, reconnaissance tools are essential for gathering information about the target system or application, much like intelligence-gathering tools for understanding the enemy's terrain.

Tools like Recon-ng and theHarvester help bug hunters collect valuable data, such as subdomains, email addresses, and publicly available information about the target.

This reconnaissance phase is critical for understanding the attack surface and potential entry points for a bug hunter, similar to a detective gathering clues to solve a case.

Exploitation frameworks are another vital category of bug hunting tools, serving as the weapons in a bug hunter's arsenal, similar to firearms in a soldier's kit.

These frameworks include tools like Metasploit, which provide a range of exploits and payloads to compromise vulnerable systems.

Bug hunters use these tools to test the severity of identified vulnerabilities by attempting to exploit them, much like a warrior testing the defenses of a fortress.

Payload generators, which are often integrated with exploitation frameworks, help create customized payloads for delivering exploits, similar to crafting specialized projectiles for a particular mission.

When conducting manual testing and analysis, reverse engineering tools become indispensable for dissecting and understanding the inner workings of applications or binaries, akin to deciphering encoded messages.

Tools like Ghidra and IDA Pro assist bug hunters in examining the source code or assembly language of applications to identify vulnerabilities and weaknesses.

These tools are particularly useful when dealing with proprietary or closed-source software, similar to solving puzzles with missing pieces.

In the realm of web application security, proxy tools like Burp Suite and OWASP ZAP are essential companions for bug hunters, acting as intermediaries between the browser and the target application, much like interpreters translating languages.

These tools allow bug hunters to intercept, inspect, and manipulate HTTP requests and responses, helping them identify security flaws and vulnerabilities in web applications.

With the increasing importance of mobile applications, mobile app assessment tools have become crucial for bug hunters, similar to specialized equipment for exploring new terrains.

Tools like MobSF (Mobile Security Framework) and Frida assist bug hunters in analyzing the security of Android and iOS applications, uncovering vulnerabilities unique to the mobile ecosystem.

When it comes to code analysis and static analysis, code review tools like SonarQube and Checkmarx are invaluable for identifying vulnerabilities in source code, similar to proofreading a manuscript for errors.

These tools automatically analyze codebases for security issues, such as code injection, insecure authentication, and sensitive data exposure.

For dynamic analysis and runtime testing, bug hunters turn to dynamic application security testing (DAST) tools like OWASP ZAP and Netsparker, which assess web applications while they are running, much like evaluating a performance on a live stage.

These tools simulate real-world attacks and identify vulnerabilities that may not be evident in static analysis.

In the domain of wireless security, Wi-Fi assessment tools like Aircrack-ng and Wireshark are essential for identifying and exploiting vulnerabilities in wireless networks, much like radio operators tuning in to different frequencies.

These tools help bug hunters test the security of Wi-Fi networks, including cracking WEP and WPA/WPA2 encryption, sniffing traffic, and detecting rogue access points.

Collaboration and reporting tools are the final piece of the bug hunting toolkit, akin to communication devices for coordinating operations.

Tools like JIRA and Confluence assist bug hunters in documenting their findings, managing vulnerabilities, and communicating with development and security teams.

They facilitate the reporting and remediation process, ensuring that identified vulnerabilities are addressed in a timely manner, much like an efficient communication network in a military operation.

In summary, bug hunting tools are essential instruments in the arsenal of cybersecurity professionals, enabling them to identify and mitigate vulnerabilities in systems and applications.

Much like a well-prepared explorer or craftsman, bug hunters rely on a diverse set of tools to navigate the intricate landscape of cybersecurity and uncover hidden weaknesses.

These tools, ranging from scanners and reconnaissance instruments to exploitation frameworks and reporting aids, empower bug hunters to uncover vulnerabilities, strengthen defenses, and ultimately enhance the security posture of the digital world.

In the world of cybersecurity, effective bug hunting strategies are the guiding principles that enable security professionals to uncover vulnerabilities and weaknesses in software, systems, and networks.

These strategies are the result of years of experience, evolving methodologies, and a deep understanding of the ever-changing threat landscape, much like battle-tested tactics in a military campaign.

Successful bug hunting begins with meticulous planning and scoping, similar to a military operation's strategic deployment.

Bug hunters define their objectives, scope, and rules of engagement, ensuring clarity and alignment with the organization's goals.

They carefully choose their targets, whether it's a web application, network infrastructure, or a specific software component, akin to selecting strategic locations in a battlefield.

Once the scope is defined, reconnaissance becomes a critical phase in bug hunting, much like gathering intelligence before launching an attack.

Bug hunters gather information about the target, such as its architecture, technologies used, and potential entry points for attackers.

This reconnaissance phase involves techniques like open-source intelligence (OSINT) gathering, network scanning, and domain analysis.

The goal is to build a comprehensive understanding of the target's attack surface, similar to knowing the layout of the battlefield.

With reconnaissance data in hand, bug hunters move on to identifying potential vulnerabilities and weaknesses, similar to finding weak points in an adversary's defenses.

They employ various techniques, including automated scanning, manual testing, and code analysis, to uncover security flaws.

This process may reveal common vulnerabilities such as SQL injection, cross-site scripting (XSS), or insecure configurations.

However, experienced bug hunters go beyond the basics, searching for obscure and complex vulnerabilities that may elude automated tools, much like skilled spies uncovering hidden secrets.

As bug hunters discover vulnerabilities, they prioritize them based on severity, potential impact, and exploitability, similar to ranking targets by importance on a battlefield.

Not all vulnerabilities are created equal, and bug hunters focus their efforts on the most critical ones that pose the highest risk to the organization.

Once prioritized, bug hunters enter the exploitation phase, where they attempt to validate the vulnerabilities by exploiting them, akin to launching targeted attacks on key positions.

This step involves crafting exploits, if necessary, and testing their effectiveness.

Bug hunters aim to demonstrate the impact of a vulnerability, whether it's gaining unauthorized access, exfiltrating sensitive data, or compromising the target system.

Throughout the exploitation phase, bug hunters follow ethical guidelines and avoid causing harm, much like adhering to rules of engagement in warfare.

As vulnerabilities are confirmed and validated, bug hunters document their findings in detail, much like military intelligence officers reporting on enemy movements.

The documentation includes information about the vulnerability, its impact, steps to reproduce, and potential mitigations.

Clear and comprehensive documentation is essential for effectively communicating the findings to the organization's stakeholders.

The final phase of bug hunting involves reporting and remediation, similar to addressing security breaches and fortifying defenses after a successful military operation.

Bug hunters create detailed reports that provide stakeholders with a clear understanding of the discovered vulnerabilities and their implications.

These reports often include recommendations for mitigation and remediation, helping organizations prioritize and address the identified security issues.

Bug hunters collaborate with development and IT teams to ensure that vulnerabilities are patched and mitigated, similar to coordinating efforts to secure a conquered territory.

In addition to these core bug hunting strategies, there are several principles and best practices that guide bug hunters in their quest for vulnerabilities.

Continuous learning and staying updated with the latest attack techniques and security trends are fundamental, much like military personnel undergoing ongoing training.

Bug hunters often participate in capture the flag (CTF) challenges, read security research, and attend conferences to sharpen their skills.

Moreover, collaboration and information sharing within the bug hunting community are critical, similar to intelligence sharing among allied forces.

Bug hunters frequently exchange knowledge, share experiences, and collaborate on challenging security issues.

This collective effort strengthens the overall security ecosystem.

Another key principle in bug hunting is maintaining a responsible and ethical approach, akin to adhering to international laws of warfare.

Bug hunters operate within legal boundaries, obtain proper authorization, and follow ethical guidelines to ensure their activities are lawful and respectful of privacy.

Furthermore, bug hunters understand the importance of responsible disclosure, reporting vulnerabilities to organizations in a timely and responsible manner, much like offering a fair warning before launching an attack.

Effective bug hunting strategies also emphasize the value of creativity and thinking outside the box.

Security professionals often encounter unique and unconventional vulnerabilities that require creative solutions.

They approach each assessment with a hacker's mindset, exploring uncharted territories and considering unexpected attack vectors.

In summary, effective bug hunting strategies are the foundation of successful cybersecurity efforts, much like well-planned military campaigns.

These strategies encompass meticulous planning, reconnaissance, vulnerability discovery, prioritization, exploitation, documentation, reporting, and collaboration. Bug hunters adhere to ethical principles, maintain continuous learning, and embrace creativity to stay ahead of evolving threats.

Their dedication and expertise play a vital role in safeguarding digital landscapes from potential adversaries, ensuring that organizations can defend their assets and protect against ever-evolving cyber threats.

BOOK 3
ADVANCED BUG BOUNTY HUNTING
MASTERING THE ART OF CYBERSECURITY

ROB BOTWRIGHT

Chapter 1: The Evolving Landscape of Bug Bounties

To understand the concept of bug bounties, we must take a step back and delve into the historical perspective of this innovative approach to cybersecurity.

The roots of bug bounties can be traced back to the early days of the internet when it was still an emerging and rapidly evolving technology, much like the wild frontier of uncharted territories.

In those early years, software and web applications were being developed at a breakneck pace, akin to pioneers racing to stake their claims in a new land.

With this rapid development came an inevitable consequence — a myriad of vulnerabilities and security weaknesses hidden within the code and architecture, similar to undiscovered dangers in an untamed wilderness.

As the internet grew, so did the risks associated with it, with malicious hackers and cybercriminals recognizing the potential for exploiting these vulnerabilities for personal gain, much like outlaws seeking to exploit vulnerabilities in a lawless land.

The term "bug bounty" itself harkens back to the days when software defects or errors were commonly referred to as "bugs," reminiscent of pests that infested the wilderness.

It was in this environment that the concept of bug bounties began to take shape, as organizations realized the need for a proactive approach to identifying and addressing security flaws, similar to settlers forming community watch groups to protect their homes.

One of the earliest recorded instances of a bug bounty program can be traced back to the late 1980s when a company called Hunter & Ready offered a reward for finding security vulnerabilities in its operating system, VAX/VMS, much like a town offering a bounty for capturing a notorious outlaw.

This initiative was a pioneering effort in the world of cybersecurity, setting the stage for what would eventually become a widespread and transformative practice.

However, it wasn't until the late 1990s and early 2000s that bug bounty programs gained more significant traction, akin to the growth of organized law enforcement in the untamed West.

The growth of the internet and the proliferation of e-commerce brought about an increased need for secure online transactions, similar to the need for safe trade routes in frontier towns.

During this time, companies like Netscape Communications and Microsoft began experimenting with various forms of vulnerability reward programs, offering financial incentives to security researchers who discovered and reported security issues in their software.

These early programs laid the groundwork for the bug bounty landscape we see today, similar to the formation of the first law enforcement agencies in developing towns.

In 2004, a pivotal moment occurred in the history of bug bounties when the Mozilla Foundation launched its Mozilla Security Bug Bounty Program, offering rewards to those who identified and reported security vulnerabilities in Firefox, much like deputizing individuals to help maintain law and order.

This move by Mozilla marked a significant shift in the perception of bug bounties, as it introduced the concept to a broader audience and encouraged collaboration between security researchers and software developers.

As the years passed, bug bounty programs continued to evolve, much like the maturation of a frontier town into a thriving city.

Companies across various industries recognized the value of harnessing the collective expertise of the global security community to improve their products' security.

Major tech giants like Google, Facebook, and Apple established bug bounty programs, offering substantial rewards for reporting vulnerabilities, similar to wealthy landowners investing in the development of their territories.

These programs not only provided financial incentives but also helped foster a culture of responsible disclosure and collaboration within the cybersecurity community, similar to the cooperation between settlers in a burgeoning town.

In recent years, bug bounty platforms and marketplaces have emerged, serving as intermediaries that connect organizations with security researchers, akin to trading posts in a growing frontier.

These platforms facilitate the discovery and resolution of security issues by streamlining the process of reporting and compensating researchers.

Today, bug bounties have become an integral part of the cybersecurity landscape, much like law enforcement agencies in modern cities.

They have matured into sophisticated programs with well-defined rules of engagement, clear communication channels, and substantial rewards.

Bug bounty hunters, or ethical hackers, actively participate in these programs, identifying vulnerabilities in software, web applications, and even hardware devices, akin to protectors of the digital realm.

The impact of bug bounties extends beyond the organizations that host them, as they contribute to the overall improvement of software security standards, similar to the establishment of safety regulations in industrialized societies.

The practice of responsible disclosure, encouraged by bug bounty programs, ensures that vulnerabilities are addressed promptly, reducing the risk of exploitation by malicious actors, much like the enforcement of laws in a civilized society.

In summary, bug bounties have a rich historical perspective that parallels the growth and development of the internet and the cybersecurity landscape.

What began as a modest initiative to identify and address software vulnerabilities has evolved into a global movement that harnesses the collective expertise of ethical hackers to enhance digital security.

Bug bounties have played a pivotal role in shaping the way organizations approach cybersecurity and have contributed to the establishment of responsible disclosure practices, ensuring a safer and more secure online environment for all.

In the ever-evolving landscape of cybersecurity, bug bounties have become a vital tool for organizations to identify and address vulnerabilities in their software, systems, and networks.

However, as the digital world continues to advance, bug bounty programs face a range of challenges and trends that shape their effectiveness and impact.

One of the primary challenges in modern bug bounties is the sheer volume of vulnerabilities and reports submitted by security researchers, similar to a flood of information in an information age.

As organizations expand their bug bounty programs, they receive an increasing number of submissions, requiring efficient triage and response processes to handle the influx.

This challenge highlights the need for robust program management and the development of effective workflows to sift through the reports and prioritize remediation efforts.

Another challenge lies in the complexity of software and systems, similar to the intricate architecture of a modern city.

As technology advances, software becomes more sophisticated, incorporating numerous components, APIs, and dependencies.

This complexity creates a larger attack surface, making it challenging to identify and mitigate all potential vulnerabilities effectively.

Bug hunters must possess a deep understanding of these complex systems to uncover hidden flaws, much like detectives solving intricate mysteries.

Moreover, the evolving threat landscape presents a significant challenge for bug bounty programs, similar to the emergence of new criminal tactics in a changing society.

Malicious actors are constantly innovating and developing new attack techniques, making it essential for bug bounty programs to adapt and stay ahead of these threats.

Programs must continually update their rules of engagement, encourage the exploration of emerging technologies, and incentivize researchers to focus on evolving attack vectors.

The global nature of bug bounty programs introduces a unique challenge related to compliance with international laws and regulations, similar to navigating diplomatic relations between countries.

Organizations operating bug bounty programs must ensure that their initiatives comply with legal frameworks and data protection regulations in various regions.

This challenge involves managing the legal complexities of offering rewards to security researchers while safeguarding sensitive data.

Ethical considerations also play a crucial role in modern bug bounty programs, much like the moral compass guiding societal values.

Bug hunters are expected to adhere to strict ethical guidelines when conducting assessments, avoiding any actions that could cause harm, disrupt services, or compromise privacy.

Maintaining this ethical balance is essential to preserving the integrity of bug bounty programs.

In the realm of trends, one notable shift is the increasing adoption of private bug bounty programs, akin to gated communities in a digital landscape.

Private programs restrict access to a select group of researchers, often those who have demonstrated their expertise through previous submissions.

These programs offer organizations more control over their security assessments and provide a higher level of confidentiality.

Crowdsourced security testing platforms have also gained popularity, similar to marketplaces where talent is matched with demand.

These platforms connect organizations with a global network of security researchers, streamlining the process of vulnerability discovery and reporting.

Moreover, bug bounty programs are no longer limited to traditional software and web applications, much like the expansion of urban areas into previously untouched landscapes.

They now encompass a wide range of technologies, including internet of things (IoT) devices, blockchain, and even hardware components.

This trend reflects the growing recognition that vulnerabilities can exist in virtually any digital asset.

The use of automation and machine learning is another prominent trend in bug bounty programs, similar to the automation of various tasks in modern society.

Organizations are incorporating AI-driven tools to assist in the identification of vulnerabilities, optimize the triage process, and enhance program efficiency.

These technologies augment the capabilities of bug hunters and help organizations address security issues more rapidly.

The role of bug hunters is evolving, as they are increasingly viewed as security partners rather than adversaries, much like the transformation of law enforcement into community-oriented policing.

Organizations are recognizing the value of collaborating with security researchers, offering them greater visibility, and involving them in the decision-making process.

This trend fosters a sense of community and mutual respect within the bug bounty ecosystem.

In summary, bug bounty programs continue to evolve in response to the challenges and trends shaping the cybersecurity landscape.

Efficient triage processes, complex software systems, evolving threats, legal compliance, and ethical considerations are among the challenges organizations must navigate.

Meanwhile, trends such as private programs, crowdsourced testing, expanded technology scope, automation, and collaborative partnerships with bug hunters are shaping the future of bug bounty programs.

As organizations embrace these challenges and trends, bug bounties will remain a critical tool in securing digital environments and mitigating emerging threats.

Chapter 2: Advanced Vulnerability Discovery Techniques

In the realm of cybersecurity and bug hunting, the technique known as fuzzing and automated discovery has emerged as a powerful and innovative approach to identifying vulnerabilities and weaknesses in software and systems.

Fuzzing, also known as fuzz testing or fuzzing testing, is a methodology that involves the automated generation of a vast array of random or semi-random data inputs, similar to casting a wide net to catch various types of fish.

These inputs are then fed into a target software or system to observe its behavior, much like testing the waters to see how they respond.

The goal of fuzzing is to discover unexpected or anomalous behavior that could indicate vulnerabilities, security flaws, or weaknesses, much like uncovering hidden treasure in uncharted territory.

Automated discovery, on the other hand, refers to the use of tools and scripts that systematically analyze and test software or systems, often in a methodical and structured manner, akin to conducting a thorough investigation.

While fuzzing primarily focuses on generating random inputs, automated discovery encompasses a broader range of testing techniques, including static analysis, dynamic analysis, and penetration testing, to name a few.

Together, fuzzing and automated discovery form a dynamic duo that plays a crucial role in uncovering vulnerabilities and enhancing cybersecurity, much like a skilled detective and a forensic scientist working together to solve a complex case.

The concept of fuzzing dates back to the 1980s when it was initially developed as a method to test the robustness and resilience of software against unexpected inputs, reminiscent of a stress test for a bridge.

Over the years, fuzzing has evolved and matured into a sophisticated technique that is widely used by security researchers, software developers, and organizations to proactively identify and mitigate vulnerabilities.

One of the primary advantages of fuzzing and automated discovery is their ability to identify vulnerabilities in software before they can be exploited by malicious actors, similar to identifying weak points in a fortress before an attack.

By subjecting software to a barrage of unexpected inputs, fuzzing can trigger crashes, exceptions, or abnormal behaviors that indicate the presence of a vulnerability, much like a smoke detector alerting residents to a fire.

These vulnerabilities can encompass a wide range of issues, including buffer overflows, memory leaks, data validation errors, and more, similar to different types of structural weaknesses in a building.

Once a vulnerability is discovered through fuzzing or automated discovery, the responsible party, whether it's a software developer or a security researcher, can take appropriate action to remediate the issue, similar to strengthening a structure's weak points.

This might involve patching the software, reconfiguring security settings, or implementing other mitigations, much like reinforcing a building's foundation or installing security measures.

Fuzzing and automated discovery are particularly valuable for uncovering so-called "zero-day vulnerabilities," which are vulnerabilities that are unknown to the software developer or the public, much like hidden traps that have not been detected.

These vulnerabilities can be highly sought after by malicious actors because they offer a significant advantage in launching successful attacks, similar to discovering a secret passage into a fortress.

By proactively identifying and addressing zero-day vulnerabilities through fuzzing and automated discovery, organizations can reduce their exposure to potential threats, much like fortifying a stronghold against potential invaders.

The process of fuzzing involves the creation of test cases or inputs that are designed to stress the target software in various ways, much like simulating different types of weather conditions to test a building's resilience.

These test cases are typically generated using algorithms that manipulate data inputs randomly or systematically, similar to trying different keys to unlock a door.

As the test cases are fed into the software, the goal is to identify inputs that cause unexpected behavior, such as crashes, hangs, or other anomalies, much like noticing unusual patterns in a building's structure.

Fuzzing tools and frameworks play a pivotal role in automating this process, allowing for the efficient and systematic testing of software, similar to using specialized equipment to inspect a structure for weaknesses.

There are several different types of fuzzing techniques, including:

File Fuzzing: This involves testing how a software application handles unexpected or malformed file inputs, similar to examining how a building withstands unusual environmental conditions.

Protocol Fuzzing: Protocol fuzzing focuses on analyzing how software handles unexpected or malformed network protocol data, much like testing how a building's security systems respond to breaches.

Web Fuzzing: Web fuzzing targets web applications and services, sending a barrage of HTTP requests with various payloads to uncover security vulnerabilities, similar to testing access points in a fortress.

API Fuzzing: API fuzzing focuses on testing the behavior of application programming interfaces (APIs) by sending unexpected inputs and monitoring the responses, akin to testing the reliability of communication systems.

In-Memory Fuzzing: In-memory fuzzing involves manipulating data structures and memory contents within a running software application to uncover vulnerabilities, much like assessing the stability of a building's structural components.

Automated discovery, as mentioned earlier, extends beyond fuzzing to encompass a broader range of testing techniques.

Static analysis, for example, involves examining the source code or binary code of software to identify potential vulnerabilities, similar to inspecting architectural plans for structural weaknesses.

Dynamic analysis involves running software in controlled environments while monitoring its behavior, much like conducting controlled experiments to observe reactions.

Penetration testing, on the other hand, simulates real-world attacks on software or systems to identify vulnerabilities and assess their potential impact, similar to staging mock invasions of a fortress to test its defenses.

The combination of these techniques, along with fuzzing, forms a comprehensive approach to automated discovery that allows organizations to identify and remediate vulnerabilities effectively, much like a holistic approach to ensuring the security and integrity of a structure.

In recent years, the adoption of fuzzing and automated discovery has grown significantly, driven by the increasing complexity of software and the relentless evolution of the threat landscape, similar to the growing importance of security measures in an interconnected world.

Bug bounty programs often incentivize security researchers to utilize fuzzing and automated discovery techniques to identify vulnerabilities in software and systems, much like rewarding vigilant citizens for reporting suspicious activities in a community.

Moreover, the open-source community has played a significant role in the development of fuzzing tools and frameworks, making these techniques more accessible to a broader audience, similar to collaborative efforts to improve public safety.

As organizations continue to rely on software and digital systems for critical functions, the role of fuzzing and automated discovery in ensuring cybersecurity will only become more prominent, much like the importance of maintaining the structural integrity of buildings in a modern society.

In summary, fuzzing and automated discovery represent essential tools in the cybersecurity arsenal, enabling organizations and security researchers to proactively identify and address vulnerabilities in software and systems.

These techniques, rooted in the principles of systematic testing and observation, help protect digital landscapes from potential threats and contribute to the ongoing evolution of cybersecurity practices, much like the continuous improvement of safety measures in our physical world.

In the realm of cybersecurity and bug hunting, one of the most intriguing and often overlooked aspects is the exploitation of niche vulnerabilities.

These vulnerabilities, often unique or rare in nature, can pose significant risks and challenges to organizations and their digital assets, similar to hidden weaknesses in a fortress's defenses.

Unlike common vulnerabilities that are well-documented and widely understood, niche vulnerabilities dwell in the shadows, awaiting discovery by astute security researchers and malicious actors alike.

The term "niche vulnerability" encompasses a broad range of security weaknesses that are not part of the typical repertoire of well-known vulnerabilities, much like rare and exotic species in the animal kingdom.

These vulnerabilities may arise from obscure software configurations, esoteric hardware components, unconventional use cases, or unconventional interactions between different technologies, similar to rare phenomena in nature.

One characteristic of niche vulnerabilities is their limited scope and impact, akin to the way certain insects only inhabit specific ecosystems.

These vulnerabilities often affect a narrow range of systems, applications, or devices, making them less appealing targets for attackers seeking widespread compromise.

However, their limited scope does not diminish their potential for harm, as they can still be leveraged to target specific individuals, organizations, or industries, similar to a precision strike against a high-value target.

One example of a niche vulnerability is a "one in a million" software misconfiguration that allows unauthorized access to a critical system, reminiscent of discovering a hidden passage into a well-guarded chamber.

Such misconfigurations may result from unusual or non-standard system settings that are rarely encountered in real-world scenarios, making them challenging to detect and exploit.

Another example of a niche vulnerability is a hardware flaw specific to a certain model or batch of devices, much like a genetic mutation that affects only a small population within a species.

These hardware vulnerabilities can be particularly elusive, as they require in-depth knowledge of the affected hardware and may involve exploiting subtle nuances in its design or manufacturing process.

Niche vulnerabilities can also emerge from the intricate interactions between different technologies, reminiscent of complex ecological relationships in nature.

For instance, a vulnerability may arise when specific software applications are used in conjunction with particular hardware components, creating a unique attack surface that is not present in standard configurations.

Navigating the landscape of niche vulnerabilities requires a combination of creativity, expertise, and persistence, similar to exploring uncharted territories.

Security researchers who specialize in discovering and exploiting niche vulnerabilities often possess a deep understanding of the technologies they investigate, much like field biologists who study specific ecosystems.

They must think outside the box, experiment with unconventional approaches, and meticulously analyze complex systems to uncover these hidden weaknesses.

Moreover, the process of discovering and exploiting niche vulnerabilities can be akin to solving intricate puzzles or unraveling mysteries.

Security researchers must piece together fragments of information, connect disparate dots, and uncover the underlying causes of obscure issues, much like detectives piecing together clues to solve a complex case.

One of the challenges in dealing with niche vulnerabilities is the lack of readily available information and resources, similar to the scarcity of documentation about rare species.

Since these vulnerabilities are not widely known or understood, there may be limited guidance, tools, or remediation strategies available to address them.

This scarcity of information can pose challenges for both security researchers and organizations seeking to protect their systems.

Additionally, the impact of niche vulnerabilities may be underestimated, leading organizations to overlook potential risks, much like underestimating the ecological importance of rare species in maintaining ecosystem balance.

To address this challenge, it is essential for security researchers to share their findings and insights with the broader cybersecurity community, similar to ecologists documenting the behavior and habitat of rare species.

Collaboration and knowledge sharing can help raise awareness about niche vulnerabilities, foster the development of mitigation strategies, and ultimately enhance the overall security posture of organizations.

Furthermore, organizations must adopt a proactive and adaptive approach to security to defend against potential niche vulnerabilities, similar to conservation efforts to protect endangered species.

This includes conducting thorough security assessments, monitoring for unusual behavior, and staying informed about emerging threats.

In some cases, organizations may need to customize their security measures to account for specific risks associated with niche vulnerabilities, similar to tailoring conservation strategies to protect rare species.

Ultimately, the exploitation of niche vulnerabilities serves as a reminder that the ever-evolving landscape of cybersecurity is replete with hidden dangers and surprises, similar to the unpredictability of the natural world.

Just as ecologists continuously discover new species and ecosystems, security researchers will continue to unearth novel vulnerabilities and attack vectors.

Embracing the challenge of niche vulnerabilities requires vigilance, adaptability, and a willingness to explore the unknown, much like the spirit of discovery that drives both scientific exploration and cybersecurity research.

In summary, the world of niche vulnerabilities is a captivating and complex realm within the field of cybersecurity.

These vulnerabilities, characterized by their uniqueness and limited scope, present both challenges and opportunities for security researchers and organizations.

Navigating this landscape requires a blend of expertise, creativity, and collaboration, similar to the exploration of uncharted territories in the natural world.

As the digital landscape continues to evolve, the hunt for niche vulnerabilities will remain a vital aspect of cybersecurity, reminding us of the hidden intricacies that define the realm of digital security.

Chapter 3: Cryptographic Flaws and Advanced Exploitation

In the realm of cybersecurity, the world of cryptographic protocols stands as a formidable fortress guarding sensitive information and communications, much like an impregnable castle protecting its treasures.

These protocols, designed to secure data and ensure privacy, play a crucial role in safeguarding digital interactions in an increasingly interconnected world.

However, just as a skilled thief seeks to crack the defenses of a well-guarded castle, cyber adversaries continuously strive to exploit vulnerabilities in cryptographic protocols.

Cracking cryptographic protocols is no small feat and demands a deep understanding of mathematics, computer science, and cryptography, similar to the expertise required to decipher ancient codes and ciphers.

Cryptographic protocols serve as the foundation of secure communication on the internet, allowing individuals and organizations to exchange information while keeping it confidential and ensuring its integrity, much like a secret code that only the intended recipient can decipher.

One of the fundamental goals of cryptographic protocols is to establish trust in a digital environment, similar to the way trust is built through face-to-face interactions in the physical world.

To achieve this, these protocols employ various cryptographic techniques, including encryption, digital signatures, and key exchange algorithms, much like crafting intricate locks and keys to secure valuable possessions.

Encryption, a cornerstone of cryptographic protocols, transforms plain text into ciphertext using mathematical algorithms, rendering the information unreadable to unauthorized parties, akin to sealing a letter in an envelope before sending it.

Digital signatures, on the other hand, provide a means of verifying the authenticity and integrity of digital messages or documents, much like an official seal on a document.

Key exchange algorithms enable secure sharing of cryptographic keys between parties, ensuring that only authorized entities can decrypt and access sensitive data, similar to a secure exchange of keys for a vault.

Despite the robustness of cryptographic protocols, vulnerabilities can emerge due to various factors, including flawed implementation, inadequate key management, or advancements in computational power, reminiscent of a crack in the walls of a castle due to wear and tear.

One common approach to cracking cryptographic protocols is through brute force attacks, where an adversary systematically tries all possible combinations of keys or inputs, much like attempting to open a lock by trying every conceivable combination.

To defend against brute force attacks, cryptographic protocols often use keys that are sufficiently long to make exhaustive searches infeasible, similar to using a complex lock with a large number of possible combinations.

However, advancements in computing power, such as the development of quantum computers, pose a potential threat to the security of cryptographic protocols, similar to the invention of a new, more advanced siege weapon.

Quantum computers have the potential to solve certain mathematical problems, like integer factorization, which underpins some widely used encryption algorithms, much like a siege weapon that can breach previously impenetrable defenses.

To address this emerging threat, researchers are exploring quantum-resistant cryptographic protocols that can withstand attacks by quantum computers, akin to fortifying castle walls to withstand new weapons.

Another avenue for cracking cryptographic protocols involves exploiting implementation flaws or vulnerabilities in the software or hardware that implements these protocols, similar to discovering a secret passage into a castle through a hidden tunnel.

These implementation flaws may enable attackers to intercept or manipulate encrypted communications, bypass authentication mechanisms, or gain unauthorized access to sensitive data, much like infiltrating a castle by exploiting a hidden entrance.

To mitigate implementation vulnerabilities, rigorous security assessments, code reviews, and penetration testing are essential, much like conducting thorough inspections of a castle's defenses to identify weak points.

Moreover, cryptographic protocols may be susceptible to attacks that exploit weaknesses in the underlying mathematical algorithms or cryptographic primitives, reminiscent of undermining a castle's foundations.

For example, vulnerabilities like the "Heartbleed" bug in the OpenSSL library highlighted the importance of addressing issues at the algorithmic level, similar to reinforcing a castle's foundations to prevent structural weaknesses.

Furthermore, cryptographic protocols must contend with the ever-evolving landscape of cyber threats and attacks, much like a castle facing constant attempts to breach its defenses.

As attackers develop new techniques and strategies, cryptographic protocols must adapt to maintain their security, similar to fortifying a castle against evolving siege tactics.

The study of cryptographic vulnerabilities and the development of secure cryptographic protocols are ongoing endeavors, much like the continuous improvement of castle defenses throughout history.

Security researchers and cryptographers collaborate to identify potential weaknesses, devise stronger algorithms, and enhance the implementation of cryptographic protocols, similar to medieval architects and engineers working to fortify castles against new threats.

In the quest to crack cryptographic protocols, the adversary's motivation can vary, ranging from espionage and data theft to identity theft and financial fraud, similar to the diverse motivations of historical castle attackers, including conquerors, thieves, and spies.

As the digital world becomes increasingly interconnected and reliant on secure communication, the importance of cryptographic protocols cannot be overstated, much like the critical role of castles in safeguarding territories throughout history.

Organizations and individuals must remain vigilant in the face of emerging threats and vulnerabilities, continuously updating and fortifying their cryptographic defenses, akin to the constant vigilance and maintenance required to protect a castle from potential adversaries.

In summary, the world of cryptographic protocols is a complex and dynamic realm in the field of cybersecurity.

These protocols form the bedrock of secure communication in the digital age, much like the robust fortifications that protected valuable assets in the past.

While cracking cryptographic protocols presents formidable challenges, ongoing research and collaboration are essential to stay ahead of potential threats and ensure the continued security of digital interactions.

In the realm of cybersecurity, advanced crypto-related exploits represent a sophisticated and intricate branch of digital attacks, akin to the subtle maneuvers of a master thief navigating a complex web of security systems.

These exploits leverage vulnerabilities in cryptographic systems, cryptographic protocols, or the way cryptography is implemented, much like infiltrating a heavily guarded facility by exploiting weaknesses in its surveillance and access control systems.

To understand advanced crypto-related exploits, it's essential to first grasp the critical role cryptography plays in securing digital communications, similar to recognizing the importance of intricate locks and keys in safeguarding valuable assets.

Cryptography serves as the science and practice of concealing information and ensuring its integrity, much like encoding messages in secret languages to keep them safe from prying eyes.

One of the fundamental aspects of cryptography is encryption, a process that transforms plaintext into ciphertext using mathematical algorithms, rendering the information indecipherable to anyone without the corresponding decryption key, reminiscent of sealing a message in a locked box.

In the digital world, encryption plays a pivotal role in protecting sensitive data during transmission and storage, akin to securing valuable documents in a vault.

However, the complexity and sophistication of cryptographic systems also make them susceptible to exploitation, similar to how the most elaborate security systems can still be breached by a determined intruder.

Advanced crypto-related exploits encompass a wide range of attack vectors and techniques, often involving a deep understanding of mathematics, cryptography, and computer science, much like the expertise required to craft intricate lock-picking tools.

One avenue for these exploits is the identification of cryptographic vulnerabilities in widely used algorithms, such as those used for encryption and digital signatures, reminiscent of discovering a hidden weakness in a well-known security mechanism.

Over time, weaknesses can emerge in cryptographic algorithms due to advances in computing power, the development of new mathematical attack methods, or flawed algorithm designs, similar to the way older lock designs can become vulnerable to modern lock-picking techniques.

Cryptanalysis, the science of analyzing and breaking cryptographic systems, plays a pivotal role in identifying these vulnerabilities, much like dissecting a lock to understand its inner workings.

Another realm of advanced crypto-related exploits involves vulnerabilities in cryptographic protocols, which are the rules and procedures that govern secure communication, akin to the protocols and procedures followed in a secure facility.

Exploiting protocol vulnerabilities can allow attackers to intercept, manipulate, or tamper with encrypted communications, similar to intercepting and altering messages exchanged within a secure facility.

One well-known example is the BEAST (Browser Exploit Against SSL/TLS) attack, which exploited a vulnerability in the TLS 1.0 protocol, allowing attackers to decrypt secure HTTPS connections, much like a thief intercepting and decoding secure radio communications between security personnel.

Furthermore, advanced crypto-related exploits can target the way cryptography is implemented in software or hardware, uncovering flaws or vulnerabilities that could compromise the security of cryptographic systems, reminiscent of discovering a hidden passage into a secure facility.

For instance, side-channel attacks exploit information leaked during the execution of cryptographic algorithms, such as timing information or power consumption patterns, similar to observing the habits and routines of security personnel to find vulnerabilities.

These attacks can reveal cryptographic keys or other sensitive information, undermining the security of encryption, much like uncovering the routines and habits of security personnel to exploit weaknesses in their behavior.

To defend against advanced crypto-related exploits, security professionals must employ a multi-faceted approach, much like a comprehensive security strategy in a physical facility.

This approach includes staying informed about emerging cryptographic vulnerabilities and updates, similar to regular security assessments and maintenance in a physical facility.

Moreover, organizations should use strong cryptographic algorithms, employ secure implementation practices, and follow best practices for cryptographic key management, akin to utilizing robust security measures and access control in a facility.

Additionally, encryption should be combined with other security measures, such as intrusion detection and response systems, to detect and mitigate crypto-related attacks, much like using surveillance cameras and alarms to monitor and respond to security breaches in a facility.

The study and mitigation of advanced crypto-related exploits are ongoing endeavors, similar to the constant evolution of security measures and tactics in physical security.

Security researchers and cryptographers collaborate to identify vulnerabilities, design stronger cryptographic systems, and develop countermeasures against emerging threats, much like architects and engineers continually improve security designs in physical facilities.

As the digital landscape evolves, advanced crypto-related exploits will remain a formidable challenge, underscoring the importance of ongoing research and vigilance in the field of cybersecurity, much like the perpetual quest for enhanced security in the physical world.

In summary, the world of advanced crypto-related exploits represents a complex and ever-evolving aspect of cybersecurity.

These exploits leverage vulnerabilities in cryptographic systems and protocols, demanding a deep understanding of cryptography and computer science.

As digital communications and transactions continue to grow in importance, defending against advanced crypto-related exploits remains a crucial aspect of ensuring the security and privacy of digital interactions.

Chapter 4: Network Intrusion and Advanced Privilege Escalation

In the realm of cybersecurity, advanced network attacks and intrusions stand as formidable adversaries, akin to skilled infiltrators seeking to breach the defenses of a well-guarded fortress.

These sophisticated attacks leverage vulnerabilities in network infrastructure and systems, employing intricate techniques to evade detection and gain unauthorized access, much like a stealthy operative navigating a complex web of security measures.

To understand advanced network attacks and intrusions, it's essential to first grasp the critical role of networks in modern communication and data exchange, reminiscent of the intricate networks of roads and tunnels that enable the flow of goods and information in the physical world.

Networks serve as the backbone of the digital age, facilitating the transmission of data, the operation of applications, and the connectivity of devices, much like the intricate transport systems that enable the functioning of cities.

However, the interconnected nature of networks also makes them vulnerable to exploitation, similar to the way multiple entry points into a fortress can be exploited by determined adversaries.

Advanced network attacks encompass a wide range of techniques and strategies, often requiring a deep understanding of network protocols, operating systems, and cybersecurity principles, much like the expertise required to navigate complex security systems.

One common avenue for these attacks is the exploitation of vulnerabilities in network protocols and services, reminiscent of finding a hidden entrance into a secure facility.

Network protocols, such as the Transmission Control Protocol (TCP) and Internet Protocol (IP), govern the rules and procedures for data exchange between devices on a network, much like the protocols that dictate how visitors are processed and admitted into a facility.

Exploiting vulnerabilities in these protocols can lead to attacks like Distributed Denial of Service (DDoS), where multiple compromised devices flood a target system, rendering it inaccessible, similar to overwhelming a facility's defenses with a coordinated onslaught.

Moreover, advanced network attacks often target specific services or applications running on networked devices, much like infiltrators focusing their efforts on breaching specific areas within a fortress.

For example, attackers may exploit vulnerabilities in web servers, email services, or database systems to gain unauthorized access or steal sensitive information, akin to infiltrating a facility by exploiting weaknesses in its individual components.

Furthermore, intruders may employ sophisticated techniques like zero-day exploits, which target previously unknown vulnerabilities, much like a master thief discovering a hidden passage into a fortress that has never been breached.

These zero-day exploits can bypass traditional security measures and go undetected until they are used, posing a significant threat to networked systems, similar to an undetected infiltrator within a fortress.

To defend against advanced network attacks and intrusions, organizations must adopt a multi-layered security approach, much like fortifying a fortress with walls, moats, and guards.

This approach includes implementing robust access controls, monitoring network traffic for anomalies, and promptly patching known vulnerabilities, similar to the combination of physical barriers, surveillance, and security personnel in a fortified facility.

Moreover, organizations should employ intrusion detection and prevention systems to identify and block malicious activities, much like using alarms and security personnel to respond to breaches in a facility.

Additionally, continuous security monitoring and threat intelligence are essential to detect and mitigate advanced attacks in real-time, akin to maintaining vigilant watchtowers and scouts to identify threats.

The study and mitigation of advanced network attacks and intrusions are ongoing endeavors, much like the constant evolution of security measures and tactics in physical security.

Security professionals and researchers collaborate to identify vulnerabilities, design stronger network defenses, and develop countermeasures against emerging threats, similar to the continuous improvement of security designs in fortified facilities.

As the digital landscape evolves, advanced network attacks and intrusions will continue to pose a formidable challenge, underscoring the importance of ongoing research and vigilance in the field of cybersecurity, much like the perpetual quest for enhanced security in the physical world.

In summary, the world of advanced network attacks and intrusions represents a complex and ever-evolving aspect of cybersecurity.

These attacks leverage vulnerabilities in network infrastructure and systems, demanding a deep understanding of network protocols and cybersecurity principles.

As digital communication and data exchange continue to grow in importance, defending against advanced network attacks and intrusions remains a crucial aspect of safeguarding digital assets and ensuring the integrity of networked systems.

Privilege escalation, in the realm of cybersecurity, represents a critical phase of an attacker's journey, akin to a covert operative gaining access to restricted areas within a facility.

This technique involves elevating one's level of access and control on a computer system or network, often starting with limited privileges and gradually gaining higher levels of authority, much like a spy navigating through layers of security clearance.

Understanding privilege escalation is crucial for both defenders and security professionals, as it allows them to anticipate and mitigate these sophisticated attacks, similar to fortifying a facility against potential breaches.

Privilege escalation techniques can be categorized into two main types: vertical privilege escalation and horizontal privilege escalation, each with its own distinct characteristics and objectives.

Vertical privilege escalation, also known as privilege elevation or privilege escalation of authority, involves escalating one's privileges to gain more extensive control over a system, similar to an intruder obtaining higher-level security clearances within a facility.

This type of privilege escalation aims to acquire administrator or root-level access, granting the attacker near-complete control over the compromised system or network, much like obtaining master keys to all doors in a facility.

Horizontal privilege escalation, on the other hand, focuses on acquiring the same level of privileges but for different accounts or users, often aiming to move laterally within a network, akin to a spy impersonating different personnel to access various parts of a facility.

To understand privilege escalation techniques, it's essential to delve into the various methods and vulnerabilities that attackers exploit.

One common approach is the exploitation of software vulnerabilities, such as buffer overflows or injection attacks, much like exploiting weaknesses in the physical structure of a facility.

Attackers leverage these vulnerabilities to execute arbitrary code, gain unauthorized access, and elevate their privileges, similar to infiltrating a facility by exploiting structural weaknesses.

Another technique involves the abuse of misconfigured or insecurely implemented access controls, reminiscent of exploiting unlocked doors or unguarded entry points within a facility.

Attackers may take advantage of weak permissions, misconfigured group policies, or insecure file permissions to escalate their privileges and access sensitive resources, much like using security lapses to access restricted areas.

Moreover, privilege escalation can be achieved through the manipulation of access tokens, which are used to determine a user's level of access and permissions, similar to manipulating identification badges in a facility.

Attackers may tamper with access tokens or impersonate legitimate users to gain higher privileges, much like an intruder forging identification to gain access to secure areas.

In the context of Windows systems, privilege escalation often involves the abuse of Windows services, scheduled tasks, or DLL (Dynamic Link Library) hijacking, similar to exploiting specific vulnerabilities within a facility's infrastructure.

Attackers may compromise legitimate services or tasks to execute malicious code with elevated privileges, much like infiltrating a facility by exploiting its internal processes. Furthermore, privilege escalation can be facilitated through the exploitation of misconfigurations or weaknesses in applications, such as web applications or database systems, reminiscent of finding vulnerabilities in facility management systems.

Attackers may exploit these weaknesses to gain unauthorized access to administrative panels or databases, allowing them to escalate their privileges, similar to manipulating facility management systems to access secure areas.

To defend against privilege escalation techniques, organizations must adopt a proactive and multi-layered security approach, much like fortifying a facility with multiple security measures.

This approach includes regularly applying security patches and updates to eliminate software vulnerabilities, similar to conducting maintenance and repairs to fix structural weaknesses in a facility.

Moreover, organizations should implement strong access controls, enforce the principle of least privilege, and conduct regular security audits and assessments, akin to controlling access and monitoring security measures within a facility.

Additionally, robust endpoint security solutions, intrusion detection systems, and security information and event management (SIEM) solutions can help detect and respond to privilege escalation attempts, much like surveillance cameras and alarms in a facility.

User awareness training is also essential to educate employees about the risks of social engineering and phishing attacks, similar to training facility personnel to recognize and report suspicious behavior.

In summary, privilege escalation techniques are a critical aspect of modern cybersecurity, demanding a deep understanding of vulnerabilities and methods employed by attackers.

As digital systems and networks continue to evolve, defending against privilege escalation remains an ongoing challenge, underscoring the importance of proactive security measures and continuous vigilance in safeguarding digital assets.

Chapter 5: Code Review and Binary Analysis

Static code analysis strategies are essential tools in the software development and cybersecurity landscape, serving as a critical line of defense against vulnerabilities and defects in code, much like a meticulous quality control process in manufacturing.

These strategies involve analyzing source code without executing it, aiming to identify a wide range of issues, from programming errors to security vulnerabilities, reminiscent of meticulously inspecting a product for flaws before it reaches the market.

Static code analysis plays a vital role in improving software quality, reducing development costs, and enhancing the security of applications, similar to how rigorous quality control processes result in better products.

One fundamental aspect of static code analysis is its ability to detect coding errors and programming mistakes, such as null pointer dereferences, memory leaks, or buffer overflows, much like a thorough inspection identifies defects in a product's design or construction.

By identifying these issues early in the development process, static code analysis helps developers prevent bugs from propagating further, similar to preventing flawed components from being incorporated into a product.

Moreover, static code analysis can uncover violations of coding standards and best practices, enabling teams to maintain consistency in their codebase and adhere to established coding guidelines, much like ensuring uniformity in product specifications and manufacturing processes.

Consistency in coding standards simplifies code reviews, facilitates collaboration among developers, and contributes to codebase maintainability, akin to standardized processes streamlining manufacturing and assembly in a production line.

Security is a paramount concern in software development, and static code analysis plays a crucial role in identifying security vulnerabilities, similar to conducting thorough safety inspections in a manufacturing facility.

The analysis can pinpoint issues like SQL injection, cross-site scripting (XSS), or improper input validation, helping developers patch vulnerabilities before attackers can exploit them, much like addressing safety concerns before they lead to accidents on a factory floor.

Furthermore, static code analysis assists organizations in complying with industry regulations and security standards, similar to adhering to safety and quality standards in manufacturing.

For example, it can help identify violations of security regulations like the Health Insurance Portability and Accountability Act (HIPAA) or the Payment Card Industry Data Security Standard (PCI DSS), much like adhering to specific industry standards in manufacturing processes.

Static code analysis tools employ various techniques and algorithms to analyze source code, such as abstract syntax tree (AST) analysis, data flow analysis, and taint analysis, akin to utilizing specialized tools and instruments in manufacturing inspections.

AST analysis involves parsing the source code to create a hierarchical representation of its structure, allowing the tool to understand the code's syntax and identify potential issues, similar to analyzing blueprints and schematics in manufacturing.

Data flow analysis traces the flow of data through the code to detect potential security vulnerabilities, much like tracking the flow of materials and components in a manufacturing process.

Taint analysis identifies tainted inputs and tracks their propagation, helping detect vulnerabilities like command injection or XSS attacks, similar to ensuring the integrity of materials and components throughout manufacturing processes.

The effectiveness of static code analysis largely depends on the accuracy of the analysis rules and the tool's ability to minimize false positives and negatives, much like the reliability of inspection equipment in manufacturing.

False positives occur when the tool incorrectly flags code as problematic when it is not, leading to unnecessary manual reviews and potentially wasting development time, similar to erroneous defect reports causing delays in manufacturing.

False negatives, on the other hand, occur when the tool fails to identify actual issues, leaving vulnerabilities undetected, akin to missing defects during inspections that can lead to product recalls in manufacturing.

To maximize the benefits of static code analysis, organizations must carefully configure and customize the tool to suit their specific development environment and coding standards, similar to calibrating inspection equipment to meet the requirements of a particular manufacturing process.

Static code analysis is not a one-time endeavor but an integral part of the software development lifecycle, requiring continuous integration into the development process, similar to ongoing quality control and testing in manufacturing.

Moreover, static code analysis can be integrated into the build and deployment pipeline, automatically scanning code changes and providing immediate feedback to developers, much like real-time monitoring and feedback systems in manufacturing.

In summary, static code analysis strategies are indispensable tools in modern software development and cybersecurity.

These strategies help improve code quality, reduce development costs, enhance security, and ensure compliance with industry regulations and standards, similar to how meticulous quality control processes contribute to the production of high-quality and safe products.

Dynamic analysis of binaries Is a fundamental technique in the field of cybersecurity, serving as a critical method for understanding and assessing the behavior of executable files, much like studying the actions and interactions of living organisms.

This technique involves running an executable file in a controlled environment and monitoring its behavior during execution, aiming to uncover potential security vulnerabilities, malicious activities, or unexpected behavior, similar to observing the behavior of an organism in a controlled laboratory setting.

Dynamic analysis is particularly valuable when dealing with closed-source or proprietary software, where access to the source code is limited or unavailable, much like studying a species without full knowledge of its genetic makeup.

One key aspect of dynamic analysis is its ability to reveal the runtime behavior of binaries, allowing analysts to observe how an executable interacts with the system, external resources, and user inputs, similar to studying an organism's response to stimuli and its interactions with the environment.

Dynamic analysis can identify various types of vulnerabilities and threats, such as buffer overflows, privilege escalation attempts, or malware behavior, much like a biologist identifying health issues or abnormal behavior in an organism.

By analyzing the execution of binaries, security professionals can uncover hidden malware, detect exploitation attempts, and assess the overall security posture of a system, akin to diagnosing and treating illnesses in living organisms.

One of the primary tools used for dynamic analysis of binaries is the debugger, which allows analysts to interact with the running executable, set breakpoints, and inspect the program's memory and registers, much like a scientist using specialized instruments to study an organism's internal processes.

During dynamic analysis, analysts often employ techniques like code tracing, which involves tracking the flow of execution within the binary, similar to tracing the pathways of signals within an organism's nervous system.

Code tracing helps analysts understand how a binary operates, identify potential security flaws, and assess the impact of malicious code, much like studying the neural pathways and responses of organisms.

Moreover, dynamic analysis can uncover the presence of malware by monitoring system calls and API (Application Programming Interface) calls made by the binary, akin to detecting signs of infection or disease in organisms through the observation of specific behaviors and symptoms.

By analyzing the interactions between the binary and the operating system, analysts can identify suspicious activities and malicious intent, similar to identifying the signs of illness in organisms.

Dynamic analysis also plays a crucial role in the analysis of network traffic generated by binaries, allowing analysts to trace communication with external servers, identify data exfiltration attempts, and understand the binary's network behavior, much like studying the communication and social interactions of organisms in their environment.

Additionally, dynamic analysis can help assess the binary's impact on system resources, such as memory and CPU usage, revealing resource-intensive or potentially disruptive behavior, akin to assessing the physiological effects of organisms on their ecosystem.

To effectively conduct dynamic analysis, security professionals must create controlled environments or sandboxes where binaries can be executed safely, similar to designing experiments in a controlled laboratory setting for studying organisms.

These sandboxes isolate the binary from the host system, preventing potential harm to the system and allowing analysts to observe its behavior without risking infection or compromise, much like using containment measures to ensure the safety of researchers studying organisms in a controlled environment.

While dynamic analysis is a powerful technique for uncovering security issues, it has its limitations, similar to the challenges faced by scientists studying complex organisms.

One limitation is the potential for evasion by sophisticated malware, which may detect the presence of a sandbox or analysis environment and alter its behavior to avoid detection, much like organisms evolving to evade predators or adapt to changing environments.

Moreover, dynamic analysis can be resource-intensive and time-consuming, especially when dealing with large and complex binaries, similar to the challenges of conducting long-term and resource-intensive experiments on organisms.

Furthermore, dynamic analysis may not uncover all security vulnerabilities or threats, as certain issues may only manifest under specific conditions that are not replicated in the analysis environment, much like studying organisms in captivity may not reveal their full range of behaviors in the wild.

Despite these limitations, dynamic analysis remains a vital tool in the cybersecurity arsenal, enabling security professionals to assess the behavior of binaries, detect malware, uncover security vulnerabilities, and enhance the overall security of systems and applications, much like studying organisms contributes to our understanding of life and its complexities.

In summary, dynamic analysis of binaries is a critical technique in cybersecurity, allowing analysts to observe the behavior of executable files, uncover security vulnerabilities, and detect malware.

This technique provides valuable insights into the runtime behavior of binaries, much like studying organisms helps us understand their behavior and interactions in the natural world.

While dynamic analysis has its limitations, it plays a crucial role in enhancing the security of systems and applications, similar to how scientific research on organisms contributes to our knowledge of the living world.

Chapter 6: IoT Security Challenges and Exploits

The rapid proliferation of Internet of Things (IoT) devices in today's interconnected world has brought unprecedented convenience and functionality, much like the integration of technology has transformed various aspects of our lives.

However, this proliferation has also introduced a multitude of security vulnerabilities and attack vectors, akin to new doors and windows in a building that potential intruders can exploit.

Understanding these IoT vulnerabilities and attack vectors is crucial for safeguarding the privacy, integrity, and availability of IoT devices and the data they handle, similar to securing physical access points in a facility.

One fundamental vulnerability lies in the inadequate security measures implemented in many IoT devices, much like leaving a door unlocked or a window open.

Manufacturers often prioritize functionality and time-to-market over security, resulting in devices with default credentials, weak encryption, and no or limited security updates, similar to building access points that lack proper locks or security systems.

Attackers can exploit these vulnerabilities by easily gaining access to the device, modifying its settings, or intercepting sensitive data, much like intruders exploiting unlocked doors to enter a facility.

Moreover, IoT devices often lack sufficient protection against physical attacks, such as tampering or reverse engineering, similar to buildings with vulnerable access points that can be easily breached.

Attackers with physical access to an IoT device can disassemble it, extract firmware or credentials, and potentially discover security weaknesses that can be exploited remotely, much like infiltrators exploiting physical vulnerabilities in a facility's infrastructure.

The wireless communication protocols used by IoT devices introduce another set of vulnerabilities, much like transmitting sensitive information over unsecured channels.

Many IoT devices use insecure or outdated communication protocols, making them susceptible to interception, eavesdropping, and man-in-the-middle attacks, similar to eavesdropping on unencrypted conversations within a facility.

Attackers can exploit these vulnerabilities to capture sensitive data, manipulate device communications, or inject malicious commands, much like intercepting and altering communications within a facility's network.

Furthermore, IoT devices often lack proper security mechanisms for firmware updates and patch management, much like buildings without maintenance plans and security updates.

Without the ability to apply security patches and updates, IoT devices remain vulnerable to known vulnerabilities, similar to facilities that do not undergo necessary maintenance, leading to deteriorating security.

Insecure device management interfaces represent yet another vulnerability, similar to providing unrestricted access to certain areas within a facility.

Many IoT devices feature web-based interfaces for device management that may lack authentication, authorization, or encryption, allowing attackers to gain unauthorized control over the device, similar to unauthorized access to secure areas within a facility.

Inadequate user authentication and authorization mechanisms are prevalent in IoT devices, similar to granting access to sensitive information without proper credentials or authorization.

Devices may lack robust authentication, relying on weak passwords or no authentication at all, making it easy for attackers to compromise the device, much like accessing secure areas with little or no verification.

IoT devices also face threats from botnets and malware that target their vulnerabilities, much like infections spreading through a population.

Attackers can compromise IoT devices and use them to launch large-scale distributed denial-of-service (DDoS) attacks or other malicious activities, similar to contagious illnesses spreading through a community.

Moreover, IoT devices often lack proper data encryption and protection mechanisms, similar to leaving sensitive documents exposed in a facility.

Data transmitted or stored by IoT devices may be unprotected, making it vulnerable to interception, tampering, or theft, much like leaving sensitive information unguarded within a facility.

The lack of proper security standards and regulations for IoT devices further exacerbates the problem, similar to operating a facility without established security guidelines. IoT manufacturers and developers often do not adhere to uniform security standards, leading to inconsistencies in security practices and leaving devices susceptible to a wide range of vulnerabilities.

Additionally, the sheer number and diversity of IoT devices in use today make it challenging to monitor and manage security effectively, much like trying to secure a vast and complex facility with numerous access points.

Mitigating IoT vulnerabilities and attack vectors requires a multifaceted approach, similar to implementing comprehensive security measures in a facility.

Manufacturers must prioritize security in the design and development of IoT devices, incorporating robust authentication, encryption, and update mechanisms, similar to installing strong locks and surveillance systems in a building.

Device management interfaces should be secured with proper authentication and authorization, akin to restricting access to secure areas within a facility.

Furthermore, users must be educated about IoT security best practices, including changing default credentials, keeping devices updated, and monitoring for suspicious activity, much like training personnel to recognize and report security threats in a facility.

IoT security standards and regulations need to be established and enforced, similar to implementing industry standards and guidelines for facility security.

Regular security assessments and audits of IoT devices can help identify vulnerabilities and weaknesses, much like conducting security inspections and audits in a facility.

Security professionals must continuously monitor IoT networks for signs of compromise, detect unauthorized access, and respond to security incidents promptly, akin to maintaining a vigilant security presence in a facility.

In summary, IoT vulnerabilities and attack vectors pose significant challenges to the security of interconnected devices and the data they handle.

Addressing these vulnerabilities requires a concerted effort from manufacturers, users, and regulatory bodies, similar to securing physical access points and infrastructure in a facility.

By prioritizing security, implementing best practices, and adhering to established standards, we can enhance the security of IoT devices and reduce the risks associated with their proliferation in our interconnected world.

Exploiting IoT devices in practice represents a significant concern in the field of cybersecurity, as these devices are becoming increasingly prevalent in our homes, workplaces, and daily lives, much like the widespread adoption of technology.

The proliferation of IoT devices offers attackers a vast attack surface, akin to having numerous entry points into a building that could be exploited for unauthorized access and malicious activities.

IoT devices often possess inherent security vulnerabilities, much like weaknesses in a building's physical infrastructure that can be exploited by intruders.

These vulnerabilities may include default or weak passwords, insecure communication protocols, and limited or no security updates, similar to having doors and windows that lack proper locks or security systems.

Attackers can leverage these vulnerabilities to compromise IoT devices and gain unauthorized control, much like exploiting physical access points in a building to breach its security.

One common method of exploiting IoT devices is the use of default or weak credentials, similar to using a stolen or easily guessed key to unlock a door.

Many IoT devices come with default usernames and passwords that are rarely changed by users, providing attackers with a straightforward entry point, akin to finding an unlocked door in a building.

Attackers can also exploit known vulnerabilities in IoT device firmware, much like using a crowbar to force open a door that has a weak latch.

Manufacturers may release security patches for IoT devices, but users often fail to apply these updates, leaving devices vulnerable to exploitation, similar to neglecting maintenance in a building.

Additionally, attackers can target insecure communication between IoT devices and their associated applications or cloud services, similar to eavesdropping on conversations within a building.

IoT devices may transmit sensitive data over unencrypted channels, allowing attackers to intercept and potentially manipulate this data, akin to listening in on unsecured conversations.

Furthermore, IoT devices may lack proper authentication and authorization mechanisms, similar to allowing unauthorized individuals to access restricted areas within a building.

Without robust security measures, attackers can easily gain control over IoT devices, manipulate their settings, or steal sensitive information, much like infiltrating secure areas.

IoT devices also face threats from malware and botnets, akin to the spread of diseases within a population.

Attackers can compromise IoT devices and use them to launch distributed denial-of-service (DDoS) attacks, propagate malware, or engage in other malicious activities, similar to infections spreading among individuals.

Moreover, attackers may target the physical security of IoT devices, similar to tampering with access points in a building.

By physically accessing an IoT device, attackers can extract credentials, modify firmware, or introduce malicious hardware components, much like tampering with locks and security systems.

In practice, exploiting IoT devices often involves a combination of techniques, similar to orchestrating a series of actions to infiltrate a building.

Attackers may first identify vulnerable devices, conduct reconnaissance, and select the most suitable attack vector, akin to planning a targeted intrusion.

Once a vulnerable device is identified, attackers can gain unauthorized access, execute malicious code, or intercept data, similar to infiltrating a building's security defenses.

The consequences of exploiting IoT devices can be severe, similar to the potential damage caused by unauthorized access to a building.

Attackers can compromise user privacy, steal sensitive information, disrupt device functionality, and even use compromised devices to launch attacks on other targets, much like the harm caused by security breaches in a facility.

Mitigating the risks associated with exploiting IoT devices requires a proactive and multifaceted approach, akin to implementing comprehensive security measures in a building. Manufacturers must prioritize security in the design and development of IoT devices, incorporating robust authentication, encryption, and update mechanisms, similar to installing strong locks, alarms, and surveillance systems in a building.

Users must be educated about IoT security best practices, including changing default credentials, keeping devices updated, and monitoring for suspicious activity, much like training personnel to recognize and respond to security threats in a facility. IoT security standards and regulations need to be established and enforced to ensure that manufacturers adhere to uniform security practices, similar to implementing industry standards and guidelines for building security. Security professionals must continuously monitor IoT networks for signs of compromise, detect unauthorized access, and respond to security incidents promptly, akin to maintaining a vigilant security presence in a facility. In summary, exploiting IoT devices in practice represents a significant challenge in the realm of cybersecurity, given the widespread adoption of these devices and their inherent vulnerabilities.

Addressing this challenge requires a concerted effort from manufacturers, users, and regulatory bodies, similar to securing physical access points and infrastructure in a building.

By prioritizing security, implementing best practices, and adhering to established standards, we can enhance the security of IoT devices and reduce the risks associated with their exploitation in our increasingly interconnected world.

Chapter 7: Cloud Security and Serverless Computing

Securing cloud infrastructure is a critical aspect of modern cybersecurity, as organizations increasingly rely on cloud services to store, process, and manage their data and applications.

The adoption of cloud computing offers numerous benefits, much like the advantages of outsourcing certain aspects of a business to specialized providers.

Cloud services provide scalability, flexibility, and cost-efficiency, allowing organizations to focus on their core competencies, similar to delegating specific tasks to experts.

However, the use of cloud infrastructure introduces a unique set of security challenges, akin to entrusting valuable assets to external partners.

Securing cloud infrastructure is a shared responsibility between the cloud service provider and the organization that uses these services, much like a partnership where both parties must contribute to success.

The cloud service provider is responsible for securing the underlying infrastructure, such as data centers, networking, and hardware, similar to ensuring the safety and integrity of a shared physical space.

On the other hand, the organization using the cloud services is responsible for securing its data, applications, and configurations within the cloud environment, akin to safeguarding its assets within a shared facility.

One of the primary challenges in securing cloud infrastructure is the dynamic nature of cloud environments, much like managing a constantly changing workspace.

Cloud resources can be provisioned, scaled, and decommissioned rapidly, making it challenging to maintain visibility and control, similar to managing a flexible office space with ever-shifting boundaries.

To address this challenge, organizations must implement robust identity and access management (IAM) controls, akin to issuing access cards and keys for secure access to a building.

IAM policies should define who can access cloud resources, what actions they can perform, and under what conditions, similar to specifying access rights and permissions within a facility.

Implementing strong authentication mechanisms, such as multi-factor authentication (MFA), is crucial to prevent unauthorized access, similar to requiring biometric scans or PINs for secure facility entry.

Furthermore, organizations should regularly review and audit IAM policies and access rights to ensure they align with security requirements, much like conducting security audits within a facility to identify vulnerabilities.

Another key aspect of securing cloud infrastructure is data protection, similar to safeguarding sensitive information within a secure room.

Organizations must encrypt data both in transit and at rest within the cloud environment, ensuring that even if data is intercepted or compromised, it remains unreadable, akin to using secure encryption for sensitive documents.

Moreover, cloud providers offer various encryption options, such as key management services, that allow organizations to maintain control over encryption keys, similar to securing access to a vault.

Implementing data loss prevention (DLP) solutions is essential to monitor and prevent the unauthorized sharing or leakage of sensitive data, much like implementing security cameras and alarms within a facility.

Additionally, organizations should establish data retention and disposal policies to ensure that data is retained only as long as necessary and securely deleted when no longer needed, akin to managing document archives.

Another critical aspect of securing cloud infrastructure is network security, similar to implementing robust perimeter defenses in a facility.

Organizations should implement network security groups (NSGs) or firewalls to control inbound and outbound traffic to cloud resources, much like installing security gates and fences around a property.

Regularly monitoring and analyzing network traffic is essential to detect and respond to suspicious activities, similar to having surveillance systems in place.

Implementing intrusion detection and prevention systems (IDS/IPS) can help identify and mitigate threats within the cloud environment, akin to having security personnel on patrol.

Additionally, organizations should adopt a zero-trust security model, assuming that no network or user is inherently trusted, and verifying each access request rigorously, similar to implementing strict access controls in a facility.

Securing cloud infrastructure also involves maintaining strong security hygiene for cloud configurations, much like ensuring that all doors and windows in a building are properly locked and secured.

Organizations should regularly assess and remediate misconfigurations in their cloud resources to minimize vulnerabilities, much like conducting security inspections.

Automation tools and scripts can help enforce security baselines and policies consistently, akin to using automated security systems.

Furthermore, organizations should have an incident response plan tailored to cloud environments, similar to having emergency response procedures in place within a facility.

This plan should outline the steps to take in the event of a security incident, including communication, investigation, containment, and recovery, akin to responding to security breaches.

Regularly conducting security assessments and penetration testing of cloud environments is crucial to identify vulnerabilities and weaknesses proactively, much like hiring ethical hackers to test facility security.

Moreover, organizations should stay informed about emerging threats and vulnerabilities in cloud services and update their security measures accordingly, similar to monitoring security news and adopting best practices within a facility.

In summary, securing cloud infrastructure is an ongoing and collaborative effort between organizations and cloud service providers, akin to a partnership focused on maintaining a secure environment.

By implementing strong IAM controls, data protection measures, network security, and security hygiene, organizations can mitigate the unique security challenges posed by cloud computing, similar to securing a shared physical space effectively.

Furthermore, having an incident response plan, conducting regular security assessments, and staying informed about emerging threats are essential components of a robust cloud security strategy, much like maintaining a vigilant security posture within a facility.

Attacking serverless architectures has become a prominent concern in the realm of cybersecurity, as organizations increasingly adopt serverless computing for its scalability and cost-efficiency.

Serverless computing allows developers to focus on writing code without worrying about server provisioning or management, similar to outsourcing certain tasks to specialized service providers.

However, the very nature of serverless architectures presents a unique set of security challenges, akin to navigating a maze with ever-changing walls.

One of the key challenges is the reduced attack surface, as serverless functions are designed to execute specific tasks and have limited access to system resources, much like entering a locked room with only one exit.

Attackers must find vulnerabilities within the code of serverless functions to exploit them, similar to searching for hidden weaknesses in a secure environment.

To address this challenge, organizations must implement secure coding practices for serverless functions, akin to fortifying the walls of a structure.

Developers should validate input data, avoid insecure dependencies, and follow the principle of least privilege to ensure that serverless functions have only the necessary permissions, similar to controlling who can access specific areas.

Moreover, organizations should continuously monitor serverless functions for suspicious behavior and conduct regular security assessments, much like having security patrols and inspections in place.

Another significant challenge in attacking serverless architectures is the difficulty of traditional attack vectors, such as exploiting operating systems or network vulnerabilities, similar to trying to break through a brick wall without a door.

Serverless functions are isolated from the underlying infrastructure, making it challenging for attackers to gain access to the host environment, akin to being unable to reach the inner workings of a building.

However, attackers can still target vulnerabilities within the serverless application code, such as injection attacks, authentication flaws, or insecure configurations, much like exploiting weak points in a building's design.

To defend against such attacks, organizations should implement strict input validation and output encoding, similar to preventing unauthorized access to sensitive areas.

They should also enforce strong authentication and authorization mechanisms, akin to controlling who can enter different parts of a facility.

Furthermore, organizations must secure sensitive data within serverless applications using encryption and access controls, similar to protecting valuable assets within a locked safe.

Attackers may also attempt to abuse the event-driven nature of serverless architectures, similar to trying to manipulate the flow of people or resources in a facility.

Event sources trigger serverless functions, and attackers may seek to inject malicious events or tamper with legitimate ones to cause disruptions or gain unauthorized access, much like attempting to manipulate the movements of people or resources.

Organizations should implement proper event validation and filtering to prevent malicious event injection, akin to controlling who can trigger specific actions in a building.

Additionally, monitoring and anomaly detection should be in place to identify suspicious event patterns and respond promptly, similar to having surveillance systems and alarms.

Another avenue of attack in serverless architectures is resource exhaustion, where attackers overwhelm functions with a high volume of requests, akin to creating a bottleneck in a facility.

This can lead to denial of service (DoS) or distributed denial of service (DDoS) attacks, causing disruptions and downtime, much like blocking access points in a building.

To mitigate this risk, organizations should implement rate limiting and throttling mechanisms for serverless functions, similar to controlling the flow of people or vehicles.

Moreover, organizations must be prepared to scale their serverless functions dynamically in response to increased traffic to ensure availability, akin to accommodating larger crowds in a facility.

In summary, attacking serverless architectures presents unique challenges and requires a shift in tactics compared to traditional attacks on server-based systems.

To defend against serverless attacks, organizations must adopt secure coding practices, continuously monitor for suspicious behavior, and implement strong authentication, authorization, and encryption measures.

They should also be vigilant against event manipulation and resource exhaustion attacks, ensuring that their serverless applications remain resilient and secure in an evolving threat landscape.

By understanding the nature of serverless architectures and the potential attack vectors, organizations can better defend against emerging threats in this dynamic computing environment.

Chapter 8: Evasive Bug Hunting and Stealthy Techniques

In the ever-evolving landscape of cybersecurity, avoiding detection and evading defense mechanisms has become a crucial focus for malicious actors seeking to exploit vulnerabilities and compromise systems.

Cyber attackers employ a wide range of tactics, techniques, and procedures (TTPs) to stay hidden and evade detection, much like a skilled infiltrator operating in the shadows.

One of the primary strategies used by attackers is the constant modification of their attack tools and methodologies, similar to a chameleon changing its colors to blend into its surroundings.

This tactic, known as polymorphic malware, allows attackers to create malicious code that continually changes its appearance, making it challenging for antivirus and intrusion detection systems to recognize and block.

To counter this, organizations must employ advanced threat detection mechanisms that go beyond traditional signature-based approaches, akin to developing a keen eye for subtle changes in the environment.

Behavioral analysis and machine learning can help identify patterns of suspicious behavior, even in the presence of polymorphic malware, similar to recognizing irregular movements in a familiar setting.

Attackers also leverage encryption to obfuscate their activities, encrypting communication channels and payloads to hide their intent and evade network monitoring, much like speaking in an encrypted code language.

To counter this, organizations must implement deep packet inspection and decryption techniques to inspect encrypted traffic for signs of malicious activity while respecting privacy and compliance requirements, akin to deciphering a coded message.

Furthermore, attackers often employ tactics such as "living off the land," using legitimate system utilities and tools to carry out malicious activities, similar to using everyday objects as covert tools.

This tactic makes it difficult for security solutions to distinguish between normal and malicious behavior.

Organizations should adopt a least-privilege approach, ensuring that users and processes have only the permissions and access necessary for their roles, akin to limiting access to specific tools.

By monitoring the use of these utilities and analyzing their behavior, security teams can detect unusual or suspicious activities indicative of an attacker's presence, similar to recognizing unusual behavior in a familiar setting.

Attackers also employ evasion techniques like "fileless malware," which runs malicious code directly in memory without leaving traces on disk, similar to carrying out covert operations without leaving physical evidence.

To detect and defend against fileless attacks, organizations should implement memory analysis tools and endpoint detection and response (EDR) solutions that can identify anomalous memory activity, akin to recognizing changes in a room without physical traces.

Another common evasion tactic is "sandbox evasion," where malware detects if it's running in a controlled environment, such as a sandbox, and alters its behavior to avoid detection, similar to a spy adapting to different scenarios.

To counter sandbox evasion, organizations should deploy sophisticated sandboxes that mimic real user environments and employ threat intelligence to identify malware that exhibits evasive behavior, akin to exposing deceptive tactics.

Attackers may also employ "zero-day exploits," which target vulnerabilities unknown to the vendor and, therefore, unpatched, much like discovering a hidden entrance to a secure facility.

To defend against zero-day exploits, organizations should stay vigilant for emerging threat intelligence and employ intrusion prevention systems (IPS) and vulnerability management programs, akin to reinforcing the security of known vulnerabilities.

Additionally, attackers use techniques such as "domain fronting" to hide malicious traffic behind legitimate domains, making it challenging to block malicious connections, similar to camouflaging an operation behind a legitimate business.

To mitigate this tactic, organizations should employ web content filtering, DNS analysis, and traffic anomaly detection to identify and block suspicious traffic patterns, akin to detecting unusual activities in a crowded area.

Furthermore, attackers often exploit the trust placed in digital certificates by using stolen or fake certificates to establish secure connections, similar to presenting forged identification.

Organizations should implement certificate validation processes and employ certificate transparency logs to verify the authenticity of digital certificates, akin to verifying identification documents.

In summary, avoiding detection and evading defense mechanisms has become a sophisticated and pervasive aspect of modern cyberattacks.

To effectively defend against these tactics, organizations must adopt a multi-layered security approach that combines advanced threat detection, behavioral analysis, memory analysis, and a deep understanding of emerging threats.

By staying ahead of attackers and continuously enhancing their cybersecurity posture, organizations can reduce their vulnerability to these evasion techniques and safeguard their digital assets in an ever-evolving threat landscape.

In the realm of cybersecurity, advanced evasion tactics represent the cutting edge of offensive techniques employed by malicious actors seeking to breach systems, exploit vulnerabilities, and evade detection.

These tactics involve sophisticated and highly targeted maneuvers designed to outsmart and circumvent the most advanced security measures, much like a master spy employing cunning strategies to infiltrate a secure facility.

One of the key components of advanced evasion tactics is the use of encryption and obfuscation techniques to cloak malicious activities, much like encrypting secret messages to keep them hidden from prying eyes.

Attackers leverage techniques such as steganography, where they embed malicious code or data within seemingly innocuous files or images, making it exceptionally challenging for security tools to detect, akin to hiding critical information within plain sight.

To counter these evasion tactics, organizations must implement advanced decryption and analysis capabilities that can inspect encrypted traffic and scrutinize file content for hidden threats, much like deciphering encoded messages.

Furthermore, attackers often employ the technique of "sandbox detection," wherein they deploy malware that can recognize when it is running in a controlled environment like a sandbox or virtual machine, similar to a spy detecting surveillance.

To evade sandbox detection, attackers design malware to remain dormant or exhibit benign behavior until it is executed on a real target, making it difficult for security researchers to analyze its true capabilities.

Organizations must employ deception technologies and advanced threat intelligence to identify and study new evasion techniques, akin to setting traps for adversaries and understanding their tactics.

Another advanced evasion tactic involves "fileless malware," where attackers execute malicious code directly in memory without leaving any traces on disk, much like conducting covert operations without leaving physical evidence.

To combat fileless malware, organizations should invest in endpoint detection and response (EDR) solutions that can monitor memory activity and detect anomalous behavior indicative of an attack, similar to detecting covert actions through subtle cues.

Attackers also exploit "living off the land" tactics, using legitimate system tools and utilities to carry out malicious activities, similar to a spy using everyday objects as covert tools.

To detect such tactics, organizations should employ behavioral analysis and anomaly detection techniques that can identify unusual patterns of activity, even within the realm of legitimate tools, akin to recognizing suspicious behavior in a familiar environment.

Furthermore, advanced evasion tactics often involve "DLL sideloading," where attackers place a malicious dynamic-link library (DLL) file in a trusted directory, causing a legitimate application to load and execute it, similar to a Trojan horse infiltrating a fortress.

To thwart this tactic, organizations must implement robust application whitelisting and runtime monitoring to ensure that only authorized DLLs are executed, akin to maintaining strict access control.

Attackers also leverage "anti-analysis techniques," employing a variety of measures to hinder the reverse engineering and analysis of their malware, much like a spy trying to prevent adversaries from decoding their secrets.

To counter anti-analysis techniques, organizations must invest in skilled threat researchers who can employ reverse engineering tools and techniques to dissect malware and uncover its functionality, akin to breaking through an adversary's defensive strategies.

Additionally, attackers frequently employ "in-memory injection" methods to inject malicious code directly into the memory space of a legitimate process, effectively bypassing traditional security measures, similar to infiltrating a facility by gaining access through an unsuspecting entry point.

To detect and defend against in-memory injection, organizations should implement memory protection technologies and real-time memory monitoring to identify and block suspicious memory modifications, akin to fortifying a vulnerable access point.

In summary, advanced evasion tactics represent a formidable challenge in the ever-evolving landscape of cybersecurity.

To effectively defend against these tactics, organizations must adopt a multi-faceted approach that combines advanced threat detection, behavioral analysis, memory protection, and a deep understanding of emerging threats.

By continuously staying ahead of attackers and leveraging cutting-edge technologies and expertise, organizations can enhance their cybersecurity posture and protect against advanced evasion tactics in an increasingly complex and sophisticated threat landscape.

Chapter 9: Engaging with Bug Bounty Programs Strategically

Strategic target selection is a critical aspect of offensive operations in the realm of cybersecurity, akin to a military commander carefully choosing targets in a battlefield.

This process involves identifying and prioritizing specific organizations, systems, or individuals that align with the attacker's objectives and vulnerabilities, much like selecting key targets to achieve strategic goals.

Attackers employ various strategies to select their targets, beginning with reconnaissance activities to gather information about potential victims, similar to gathering intelligence about the enemy's strengths and weaknesses.

These reconnaissance efforts include scanning the internet for vulnerable systems, profiling organizations to understand their structure and security posture, and identifying potential entry points, akin to identifying weak points in an adversary's defenses.

The goal of strategic target selection is to maximize the impact of an attack while minimizing the risk of detection and attribution, much like a general seeking to gain the upper hand in a conflict.

Attackers often favor targets with high-value assets, such as valuable data, intellectual property, or financial resources, similar to targeting enemy supply lines or command centers.

Additionally, attackers may target organizations with weak cybersecurity practices, known vulnerabilities, or limited security resources, as they offer a greater chance of success, akin to exploiting an adversary's vulnerabilities.

Attackers also consider the potential for collateral damage, assessing whether the attack might affect unintended targets or draw unwanted attention, much like military leaders weighing the consequences of their actions on civilian populations.

To protect against strategic target selection, organizations must implement robust security measures, conduct regular security assessments, and stay informed about emerging threats, similar to fortifying their defenses and maintaining situational awareness.

Furthermore, organizations should employ threat intelligence services to gather information about potential attackers and their tactics, techniques, and procedures (TTPs), akin to gathering intelligence about enemy forces.

By understanding the motivations and capabilities of potential attackers, organizations can better prepare and defend against strategic target selection.

Another aspect of strategic target selection involves the consideration of attack vectors and methods, much like choosing the appropriate weapons and tactics in a military operation.

Attackers assess the vulnerabilities and weaknesses of potential targets and select the most effective means to exploit them, similar to a military commander selecting the right strategy to overcome an adversary's defenses.

For example, an attacker might choose to use phishing emails to target employees of an organization, exploiting human weaknesses in the same way a military strategist might exploit an enemy's psychological vulnerabilities.

Alternatively, an attacker might exploit known software vulnerabilities to gain unauthorized access to a target's systems, similar to a military commander exploiting a weak point in an adversary's fortifications.

To defend against these tactics, organizations must employ a multi-layered security approach, including employee training and awareness programs, regular patch management, and intrusion detection systems, akin to fortifying their defenses against various attack vectors.

Additionally, organizations should conduct penetration testing and vulnerability assessments to identify and remediate weaknesses before attackers can exploit them, similar to a military force conducting reconnaissance and fortifying vulnerable positions.

Strategic target selection also involves the consideration of timing and the element of surprise, much like a military commander planning a surprise attack.

Attackers often choose the most opportune moment to strike, exploiting vulnerabilities when they are least expected, akin to catching an enemy off guard.

To mitigate the risk of such surprise attacks, organizations should implement continuous monitoring and threat detection systems that can identify suspicious activities and anomalies in real-time, similar to maintaining constant vigilance along potential threat vectors.

Furthermore, organizations should develop and rehearse incident response plans to ensure a rapid and effective response in the event of an attack, similar to a military unit rehearsing its response to unexpected threats.

In summary, strategic target selection is a critical component of offensive cyber operations, and attackers employ various tactics, techniques, and procedures to identify and prioritize their targets.

To defend against strategic target selection, organizations must employ robust security measures, threat intelligence services, and a multi-layered security approach that considers attack vectors, vulnerabilities, timing, and the element of surprise. By staying vigilant and well-prepared, organizations can better protect their assets and data in an ever-evolving threat landscape. Negotiation is a crucial skill in the world of bug hunting and cybersecurity, akin to the art of bargaining in various aspects of life.

It plays a pivotal role in bug bounty programs, where ethical hackers, also known as bug hunters, engage with organizations to report and remediate vulnerabilities in exchange for rewards, much like negotiating a fair deal in a marketplace. Effective negotiation can significantly impact the outcome of bug hunting engagements, ensuring that bug hunters receive fair compensation for their findings and that organizations address security issues promptly and thoroughly. One key aspect of negotiation in bug hunting is establishing clear communication with the organization running the bug bounty program, similar to open and transparent dialogue between parties in any negotiation. This communication begins with the initial report submission, where bug hunters describe their findings, the potential impact of the vulnerability, and any supporting evidence, much like presenting a case in negotiations. Clear and well-documented reports can make a significant difference in the negotiation process, as they help organizations understand the severity and scope of the vulnerability, similar to providing compelling evidence in a negotiation.

Bug hunters should also be prepared to engage in follow-up discussions with the organization, clarifying any questions or concerns and providing additional context or information as needed, akin to addressing counterarguments in a negotiation.

Effective negotiation in bug hunting involves understanding the organization's perspective, similar to empathizing with the other party's interests and concerns in a negotiation.

Organizations may have their reasons for initially assessing a vulnerability differently or proposing a specific reward amount, and bug hunters should take these factors into account during negotiations, much like recognizing the motivations and constraints of the other party in a negotiation.

Negotiating bug bounties often requires a balance between advocating for fair compensation and maintaining a cooperative and respectful relationship with the organization, similar to finding a middle ground in a negotiation to reach a mutually beneficial agreement.

Bug hunters should approach negotiations with professionalism, respect, and a focus on collaboration, as maintaining a positive working relationship can lead to future opportunities and continued engagement, much like building a long-term partnership in negotiations.

When negotiating rewards for bug hunting, bug hunters should consider several factors, such as the severity of the vulnerability, the potential impact on the organization, and the level of effort required to discover and report the issue, similar to evaluating the value and significance of concessions in a negotiation.

Bug hunters may also reference the organization's bug bounty program guidelines or industry standards to support their negotiation position, much like using benchmarks and industry norms in negotiations.

Additionally, bug hunters can highlight the importance of prompt remediation and the potential reputational damage an organization may face if a vulnerability becomes publicly known, similar to emphasizing the consequences of not reaching an agreement in a negotiation.

Effective negotiation also involves being flexible and open to compromise, similar to exploring alternative solutions and concessions in negotiations.

Bug hunters should be willing to discuss and adjust their expectations regarding reward amounts or other terms based on the organization's feedback and constraints, much like finding creative solutions and concessions to move negotiations forward.

Ultimately, successful negotiation in bug hunting results in a fair and mutually beneficial agreement between the bug hunter and the organization, similar to achieving a win-win outcome in negotiations.

Both parties should feel satisfied with the terms of the agreement, and the organization should promptly address and remediate the reported vulnerabilities, akin to fulfilling the terms of a negotiated contract.

In summary, negotiation is a fundamental skill in bug hunting, and effective negotiation can lead to fair rewards and prompt vulnerability remediation.

Bug hunters should approach negotiations with professionalism, communication, and a collaborative mindset, aiming for mutually beneficial agreements that contribute to improved cybersecurity.

Chapter 10: Building a Bug Hunting Legacy: Mentorship and Leadership

Mentoring plays a crucial role in the bug hunting community, similar to passing down knowledge and skills from experienced hunters to the next generation.

As the field of cybersecurity continues to evolve and grow, it is essential to nurture and guide emerging talent, much like an experienced mentor helping a protege develop their expertise.

Mentoring can take various forms in the bug hunting world, from one-on-one guidance to contributing to educational programs and initiatives, akin to educators and trainers shaping the skills and knowledge of their students.

Experienced bug hunters often serve as mentors, sharing their insights, experiences, and best practices with newcomers, similar to seasoned professionals providing guidance to those just starting their careers.

One of the primary roles of a mentor is to offer guidance on the fundamentals of bug hunting, much like a teacher imparting foundational knowledge to students.

This includes teaching newcomers about different types of vulnerabilities, common attack vectors, and the tools and techniques used in bug hunting, akin to laying the groundwork for a solid understanding of the field.

Mentors also help mentees develop essential technical skills, such as web application security assessment, network penetration testing, and code analysis, similar to coaches refining the techniques of athletes.

By providing hands-on training and opportunities to practice their skills, mentors prepare mentees for real-world bug hunting engagements, much like a mentor guiding an apprentice through practical exercises.

In addition to technical skills, mentors also focus on imparting soft skills that are vital in the bug hunting community, similar to mentors teaching interpersonal and communication skills to their proteges.

Effective communication, collaboration, and professionalism are crucial for bug hunters when engaging with organizations, reporting vulnerabilities, and negotiating rewards, akin to mentors shaping well-rounded individuals.

Mentoring also involves helping mentees build their online presence and reputation in the bug hunting community, much like mentors assisting proteges in establishing their identity and brand.

This includes guidance on writing clear and detailed bug reports, participating in bug bounty programs, and contributing to open-source projects, similar to mentors helping individuals stand out in their respective fields.

Mentors often encourage mentees to actively participate in bug bounty programs, similar to coaches encouraging athletes to compete in tournaments and competitions.

Bug bounty programs provide valuable real-world experience and opportunities for earning rewards, which can help mentees build their skills and gain recognition, akin to mentors guiding proteges toward success.

Furthermore, mentors play a crucial role in helping mentees navigate the bug hunting landscape, much like guides leading travelers through unfamiliar terrain.

This includes providing insights into the latest trends, emerging vulnerabilities, and best practices, similar to mentors offering valuable insights to those they mentor.

Mentors can also help mentees identify their strengths and areas for improvement, much like coaches assessing the abilities of their athletes.

By recognizing their unique talents and weaknesses, mentees can focus their efforts on areas where they can excel and seek additional support in areas where they may need assistance, akin to athletes honing their skills in specific disciplines.

Mentoring relationships often extend beyond technical guidance, similar to mentors providing personal and professional advice to those they mentor.

Experienced bug hunters may share their experiences, career insights, and strategies for success with mentees, helping them navigate the challenges and opportunities in the field, much like mentors offering life advice to their proteges.

Mentoring the next generation of bug hunters is not only beneficial for mentees but also contributes to the growth and development of the bug hunting community as a whole.

By passing on knowledge and expertise, experienced bug hunters help ensure the continuity and progress of the field, much like mentors shaping the future of their respective industries.

In summary, mentoring is a vital component of the bug hunting community, enabling experienced bug hunters to guide and support the next generation.

Through mentorship, newcomers can develop their technical and soft skills, build their reputations, and navigate the bug hunting landscape with confidence, ultimately contributing to the continued success and growth of the field.

Leadership within the bug hunting community is not solely about technical expertise but also about guiding and inspiring others.

Exemplary leaders in this field embody a combination of skills, character traits, and a commitment to the community, much like effective leaders in any domain.

One of the primary roles of a leader in the bug hunting community is to set an example for others, similar to how a captain leads a team on a journey.

Leaders demonstrate the highest standards of ethical hacking, responsible disclosure, and professionalism, inspiring others to follow suit, akin to inspiring a crew to navigate uncharted waters with integrity.

Leadership involves fostering a sense of community and collaboration among bug hunters, akin to a conductor harmonizing the efforts of individual musicians in an orchestra.

By promoting an inclusive and supportive environment, leaders encourage knowledge sharing, mentorship, and cooperation, similar to nurturing a culture of teamwork and camaraderie.

Effective leaders also play a pivotal role in advocating for ethical hacking and responsible disclosure practices, much like activists championing a cause.

They work to raise awareness about the importance of cybersecurity, educate organizations about bug bounty programs, and promote the responsible reporting of vulnerabilities, akin to advocates pushing for change and awareness in society.

In addition to advocacy, leaders contribute to the development of industry standards and best practices in bug hunting, similar to experts shaping the guidelines and regulations of their respective fields.

Their expertise and experience inform the evolution of bug bounty programs and cybersecurity protocols, ensuring that they remain effective and relevant, much like influential figures shaping the policies and regulations of their industries.

Leadership in the bug hunting community extends to the mentorship and guidance of emerging talent, much like seasoned professionals nurturing the growth of newcomers in other fields.

Experienced bug hunters often serve as mentors, sharing their knowledge and insights to help others develop their skills and navigate the complexities of bug hunting, similar to experienced mentors supporting the development of their proteges.

Leaders also lead by example when it comes to responsible disclosure, much like role models inspiring positive behavior in their communities.

They prioritize communication with organizations, report vulnerabilities promptly, and advocate for the timely remediation of security issues, akin to individuals demonstrating responsible and ethical conduct.

Effective leaders are not just technically proficient but also possess strong communication skills, similar to influential figures who can articulate their vision and ideas effectively.

They can convey complex technical concepts in a clear and understandable manner, enabling them to educate, inform, and inspire others, much like great communicators in various domains.

Leadership in the bug hunting community also involves resilience and adaptability, much like leaders who navigate challenges and uncertainties in their industries.

The cybersecurity landscape is constantly evolving, with new vulnerabilities, threats, and technologies emerging regularly, similar to industries undergoing rapid transformations.

Leaders must remain current and adaptable, continuously updating their skills and knowledge to stay ahead, akin to individuals who embrace change and innovation.

Furthermore, leaders in the bug hunting community often engage in responsible disclosure debates and discussions, much like leaders who participate in dialogues about policy and ethics.

They contribute to the ongoing conversation surrounding cybersecurity ethics, responsible hacking, and bug bounty program guidelines, similar to thought leaders shaping discussions in other fields.

Effective leadership also involves fostering a sense of community and collaboration, much like leaders who bring together diverse groups to achieve common goals.

Leaders in the bug hunting community create platforms for bug hunters to connect, share knowledge, and collaborate on projects, much like community organizers who unite individuals with shared interests.

Leadership can also extend beyond bug hunting itself, as leaders may engage in advocacy and education efforts to promote cybersecurity awareness in society, similar to individuals who use their positions to effect positive change in the world.

In summary, leadership in the bug hunting community encompasses a range of skills, responsibilities, and contributions that go beyond technical expertise.

Effective leaders inspire others, advocate for responsible hacking, contribute to industry standards, mentor emerging talent, and foster collaboration and community, ultimately shaping the evolution and impact of bug hunting in the ever-changing cybersecurity landscape.

BOOK 4
VIRTUOSO BUG HUNTER'S HANDBOOK
SECRETS OF THE ELITE ETHICAL HACKERS

ROB BOTWRIGHT

Chapter 1: The Mindset of a Virtuoso Bug Hunter

Developing a hacker's mindset is a fundamental aspect of becoming a proficient bug hunter.

It involves adopting a unique perspective and approach to problem-solving that goes beyond conventional thinking, much like a detective's ability to see patterns and clues others may overlook.

A hacker's mindset is characterized by curiosity, a thirst for knowledge, and a relentless desire to understand how systems work, akin to a scientist's curiosity about the natural world.

This mindset encourages individuals to question the status quo, challenge assumptions, and explore unconventional avenues, similar to inventors and innovators who push the boundaries of what's possible.

One of the key attributes of a hacker's mindset is the willingness to embrace failure as a learning opportunity, similar to entrepreneurs who view setbacks as valuable experiences.

In the world of bug hunting, not every attempt to find vulnerabilities will succeed, but each failure provides insights and knowledge that can be applied to future endeavors.

A hacker's mindset also involves a deep sense of persistence and determination, much like athletes who train tirelessly to achieve their goals.

Bug hunters often encounter obstacles, but their mindset propels them to keep pushing forward, seeking solutions, and overcoming challenges.

Another essential aspect of the hacker's mindset is adaptability, similar to how improvisational actors adjust to unexpected twists in a performance.

In the ever-evolving field of cybersecurity, bug hunters must be ready to pivot, learn new techniques, and adapt to emerging threats and vulnerabilities.

The hacker's mindset encourages creative problem-solving, akin to artists who explore unconventional mediums and techniques to express their ideas.

Bug hunters often devise novel approaches to discover vulnerabilities, thinking outside the box and considering scenarios that others might overlook.

A hacker's mindset values critical thinking and attention to detail, much like detectives who meticulously examine evidence to solve complex cases.

In the world of bug hunting, meticulous analysis of code, network traffic, and system behaviors is essential for identifying vulnerabilities.

Another aspect of the hacker's mindset is a strong ethical foundation, similar to the principles that guide professionals in fields like medicine and law.

Ethical hackers prioritize responsible disclosure, the protection of user data, and adherence to the law while conducting their security assessments.

Collaboration and knowledge sharing are also essential components of the hacker's mindset, much like the way scientists collaborate on research projects.

Bug hunters often work together, sharing information, techniques, and insights to collectively enhance their understanding of vulnerabilities and security.

A hacker's mindset emphasizes the importance of staying informed and continuously learning, similar to scholars who dedicate their lives to expanding their knowledge.

In the rapidly evolving world of cybersecurity, bug hunters must stay up-to-date with the latest technologies, attack vectors, and defense mechanisms.

Furthermore, the hacker's mindset embraces the responsibility to contribute positively to the security community, akin to the way mentors guide and inspire the next generation of professionals.

Experienced bug hunters often take on mentorship roles, sharing their knowledge and experiences to help others develop their hacker's mindset.

In summary, developing a hacker's mindset is a multifaceted journey that involves curiosity, adaptability, persistence, creativity, ethics, collaboration, and a commitment to continuous learning.

Bug hunters who cultivate this mindset are well-equipped to navigate the ever-changing landscape of cybersecurity, discover vulnerabilities, and contribute positively to the security community.

The psychology of a bug bounty virtuoso delves into the intricate mindset of those who have reached the pinnacle of ethical hacking excellence.

It explores the thought processes, motivations, and behaviors that set them apart from their peers, akin to a deep psychological analysis of high-achieving individuals in other fields.

At the core of a bug bounty virtuoso's psychology lies an insatiable curiosity, much like the inquisitiveness of great inventors who sought to unravel the mysteries of science and technology.

This curiosity drives them to constantly question the security of systems, searching for vulnerabilities and weaknesses that others might overlook.

A bug bounty virtuoso possesses an unrelenting drive to push the boundaries of what's possible, similar to the determination of athletes striving for world records and excellence in their respective sports.

They are motivated not only by financial rewards but also by the desire to uncover and fix vulnerabilities, making the digital world safer for everyone.

Another key element of their psychology is a keen sense of problem-solving, akin to the analytical thinking of mathematicians and physicists who tackle complex equations and theories.

Bug bounty virtuosos approach security challenges as puzzles to be solved, leveraging their technical skills and creativity to find innovative solutions.

They possess a unique ability to think like both an attacker and a defender, similar to military strategists who consider various perspectives to formulate effective plans.

This dual perspective allows them to anticipate potential threats and develop robust security measures.

One of the defining characteristics of a bug bounty virtuoso's psychology is an unwavering ethical foundation, similar to the principles that guide medical professionals and lawyers in their ethical practice.

They adhere to responsible disclosure practices, prioritize user privacy, and operate within the boundaries of the law, ensuring that their actions benefit society as a whole.

A deep sense of responsibility drives bug bounty virtuosos to use their skills for the greater good, much like philanthropists who dedicate their resources to improving the world.

Their work contributes to strengthening the cybersecurity landscape and protecting individuals and organizations from malicious attacks.

In addition to ethical considerations, the psychology of a bug bounty virtuoso includes a commitment to continuous self-improvement, similar to the dedication of scholars who pursue lifelong learning.

They stay updated on the latest security trends, hone their skills, and adapt to evolving threats, ensuring that they remain at the forefront of their field.

Bug bounty virtuosos also exhibit a remarkable level of patience, much like researchers who conduct painstaking experiments and studies.

They may spend hours, days, or even weeks meticulously analyzing code and network traffic to uncover vulnerabilities, demonstrating their unwavering determination.

Furthermore, they possess exceptional attention to detail, akin to forensic experts who scrutinize evidence to solve crimes.

Bug bounty virtuosos leave no stone unturned, meticulously examining every aspect of a system to identify potential weaknesses.

The psychology of a bug bounty virtuoso also encompasses resilience in the face of challenges, similar to individuals who overcome adversity in pursuit of their goals.

They acknowledge that not every attempt to find vulnerabilities will succeed, but they view failures as opportunities for growth and learning.

Bug bounty virtuosos often display a unique sense of community and collaboration, much like organizers who unite diverse groups around a common cause.

They actively engage with other bug hunters, share knowledge, and contribute to the collective understanding of cybersecurity.

This spirit of collaboration extends to mentoring and guiding emerging talent, similar to experienced professionals who nurture the growth of newcomers in their fields.

Experienced bug bounty virtuosos often take on mentorship roles, sharing their expertise to help others develop their skills and navigate the complexities of ethical hacking.

In summary, the psychology of a bug bounty virtuoso is characterized by curiosity, determination, ethical principles, problem-solving abilities, dual-perspective thinking, responsibility, continuous self-improvement, patience, attention to detail, resilience, community engagement, and mentorship.

Understanding the mindset of these exceptional individuals provides insights into their motivations and behaviors, shedding light on their contributions to the field of cybersecurity and the broader digital landscape.

Chapter 2: Mastering Complex Vulnerabilities and Zero-Days

Zero-day vulnerabilities are the Holy Grail of the cybersecurity world, representing undiscovered and unpatched weaknesses in software and systems.

These vulnerabilities are highly coveted by both ethical hackers and malicious actors, as they offer a unique opportunity to exploit a target without detection or defense.

The term "zero-day" refers to the fact that there are zero days of protection or mitigation available when a vulnerability is initially discovered, making it a critical and time-sensitive issue.

The allure of zero-day vulnerabilities lies in their potential for stealthy and devastating attacks, much like covert operatives who use hidden tactics to achieve their objectives.

For ethical hackers, the discovery of a zero-day vulnerability is both a thrilling and sobering moment, akin to finding a hidden treasure chest while recognizing the responsibility that comes with it.

The process of unveiling a zero-day vulnerability begins with extensive research, analysis, and testing, similar to investigative journalists who uncover hidden truths through meticulous investigation.

Ethical hackers often employ a combination of reverse engineering, code analysis, and penetration testing to identify potential zero-day vulnerabilities.

Once a potential vulnerability is identified, it undergoes rigorous testing to confirm its existence and assess its impact, much like scientific experiments that require repeated trials for validation.

The discovery of a zero-day vulnerability carries significant ethical considerations, similar to whistleblowers who expose wrongdoing while facing potential consequences.

Ethical hackers must carefully weigh the benefits of disclosing the vulnerability to the software vendor against the risks of it falling into the wrong hands.

Responsible disclosure is a core principle in the world of zero-day vulnerabilities, emphasizing the need to inform the vendor and give them an opportunity to develop a patch, much like a concerned citizen reporting a safety hazard to authorities.

The disclosure process typically follows a coordinated and confidential timeline, allowing the vendor sufficient time to create and release a patch before the vulnerability is publicly disclosed.

During this period, ethical hackers may work closely with the vendor to provide technical details and assistance in developing a fix, similar to experts advising on solving complex problems.

The responsible disclosure process is essential to protect users and prevent malicious exploitation of the vulnerability.

However, it can be a delicate and challenging process, as it requires trust, collaboration, and adherence to strict timelines, similar to negotiations between parties with conflicting interests.

In some cases, ethical hackers may receive financial compensation, recognition, or bug bounties for their responsible disclosure efforts, akin to rewards offered for valuable information.

Once a patch is developed and released, the zero-day vulnerability becomes a "one-day" vulnerability, as protections are now available.

However, the process of responsible disclosure continues, as users need time to apply the patch, and the vulnerability may remain exploitable on unpatched systems.

Malicious actors, on the other hand, are constantly seeking zero-day vulnerabilities to weaponize and use for their own gain, much like spies searching for hidden vulnerabilities to exploit.

These actors may operate in the shadows, employing advanced tactics to evade detection and leverage zero-day vulnerabilities for espionage, financial gain, or disruption.

The world of zero-day vulnerabilities is a high-stakes game, similar to a chess match between ethical hackers and malicious actors, each vying for control and advantage.

The increasing demand for zero-day vulnerabilities has given rise to a shadowy underground market where these vulnerabilities are bought and sold for significant sums of money.

This underground market operates in secrecy, resembling a black market for rare and valuable commodities.

Governments, cybersecurity firms, and intelligence agencies may also actively seek zero-day vulnerabilities for offensive or defensive purposes, much like military strategists pursuing new weapons and tactics.

The prevalence of zero-day vulnerabilities underscores the ongoing need for robust cybersecurity practices, including vulnerability management, threat detection, and incident response.

Organizations must remain vigilant, regularly update their software, and collaborate with ethical hackers through bug bounty programs to identify and address vulnerabilities before they can be exploited.

In summary, zero-day vulnerabilities are a double-edged sword in the realm of cybersecurity, offering both immense potential for protection and devastating potential for harm.

The responsible disclosure of these vulnerabilities by ethical hackers plays a crucial role in safeguarding digital ecosystems and protecting users from malicious exploitation.

As the cybersecurity landscape continues to evolve, the hunt for zero-day vulnerabilities remains a challenging and dynamic endeavor that requires a balance of technical expertise, ethical considerations, and a commitment to security.

Advanced techniques for exploiting complex flaws represent the pinnacle of ethical hacking expertise, requiring a deep understanding of software systems and intricate vulnerabilities.

These techniques go beyond the basics and delve into the realm of sophisticated attacks that target complex interactions and intricate coding errors.

The pursuit of advanced exploitation techniques parallels the quest of master craftsmen honing their skills to create works of art, as ethical hackers refine their abilities to uncover and exploit vulnerabilities.

Complex flaws often lurk beneath the surface of seemingly secure systems, much like hidden chambers in a labyrinth, and skilled ethical hackers navigate this intricate maze to discover and exploit them.

To excel in exploiting complex flaws, ethical hackers must possess a comprehensive knowledge of programming languages, system architectures, and software development processes.

They immerse themselves in the intricacies of code, searching for vulnerabilities that may result from subtle errors, misconfigurations, or unintended interactions.

Exploiting complex flaws requires a blend of technical acumen and creativity, akin to master musicians composing intricate symphonies that captivate their audience.

Ethical hackers must think beyond the obvious and devise innovative approaches to manipulate software behavior and gain unauthorized access.

One of the key aspects of advanced exploitation techniques is the ability to chain multiple vulnerabilities together, much like assembling a complex puzzle from many intricate pieces.

Ethical hackers identify and leverage multiple flaws in a sequence, each exploiting a different aspect of the system, to achieve their ultimate goal.

This chaining of vulnerabilities can be likened to an orchestration of instruments in a symphony, where each instrument contributes to the overall harmony of the composition.

The exploitation of complex flaws often requires meticulous reconnaissance and intelligence gathering, similar to espionage agents collecting vital information before executing a covert operation.

Ethical hackers must thoroughly understand the target system's architecture, protocols, and components to identify weak points and vulnerabilities.

Complex flaws may manifest as race conditions, where the timing of specific actions is critical to the success of an exploit, resembling the precision required in synchronized swimming routines.

Ethical hackers must orchestrate their actions with precision, exploiting vulnerabilities at precisely the right moment to achieve their objectives.

Exploiting complex flaws often involves bypassing sophisticated security measures and evasion techniques, much like a cat burglar eluding a high-tech security system.

Ethical hackers employ tactics such as obfuscation, injection attacks, and privilege escalation to maneuver around defenses and maintain a covert presence.

The exploitation of complex flaws can lead to advanced persistence mechanisms, where attackers establish long-term access to a system, akin to spies infiltrating enemy territory.

Ethical hackers may implant backdoors or create stealthy footholds within a compromised system, allowing them to return undetected for future attacks.

As with any advanced skill, mastering the exploitation of complex flaws requires continuous learning and adaptation, similar to martial artists refining their techniques through rigorous training.

Ethical hackers stay abreast of evolving software and security trends, adapting their methods to remain effective in an ever-changing landscape.

Exploiting complex flaws also demands a deep understanding of the consequences and impact of successful attacks, akin to military strategists considering the geopolitical implications of their actions.

Ethical hackers must weigh the potential harm and ethical considerations associated with their activities, always striving to minimize collateral damage.

Complex flaws may exist in various types of software and systems, including web applications, network protocols, and even embedded devices, presenting ethical hackers with diverse challenges.

Ethical hackers often focus on high-value targets, much like elite operatives targeting critical objectives in sensitive missions.

The exploitation of complex flaws may uncover vulnerabilities with significant implications, such as data breaches, system compromises, or even national security risks.

In summary, advanced techniques for exploiting complex flaws represent the pinnacle of ethical hacking expertise, requiring a blend of technical knowledge, creativity, and precision.

Ethical hackers who specialize in these techniques navigate the intricate world of software vulnerabilities, working tirelessly to uncover and mitigate complex flaws.

Their efforts contribute to the advancement of cybersecurity, protecting systems, data, and users from the potential harm posed by these intricate vulnerabilities.

Chapter 3: Advanced Exploitation Techniques and Artifacts

Exploiting advanced artifacts is a sophisticated aspect of ethical hacking that involves leveraging unusual or non-standard elements within software and systems.

These artifacts may not be immediately apparent, requiring a keen eye and deep technical expertise to identify and exploit effectively.

Ethical hackers who excel in this field possess a level of skill and creativity akin to detectives solving complex mysteries, as they uncover hidden vulnerabilities within software.

Advanced artifacts can manifest in various forms, including obscure configurations, rarely used features, or unexpected data flows.

To exploit these artifacts, ethical hackers must first recognize their presence, much like uncovering concealed clues in a detective story.

Identifying advanced artifacts often requires a deep understanding of the target software or system, similar to a researcher who comprehensively studies their subject.

Once an advanced artifact is identified, ethical hackers embark on a journey to understand its inner workings and potential vulnerabilities.

This process may involve reverse engineering, code analysis, or system exploration, resembling an archaeologist carefully excavating and examining ancient artifacts.

Advanced artifacts can sometimes lead to the discovery of novel attack vectors, much like uncovering hidden passageways in a labyrinthine castle.

Ethical hackers must think outside the box, employing unconventional methods and approaches to exploit these artifacts.

They may combine multiple artifacts or unconventional data inputs, much like an artist blending different colors to create a unique masterpiece.

The exploitation of advanced artifacts often requires a deep dive into the software's source code, where subtle vulnerabilities may lurk, much like uncovering hidden messages in a complex cipher.

Ethical hackers meticulously scrutinize the code, searching for weaknesses that can be leveraged to gain unauthorized access or manipulate the software's behavior.

Exploiting advanced artifacts can be akin to solving a complex puzzle, as ethical hackers piece together various elements to achieve their objectives.

These elements may include unusual data structures, unexpected interactions, or rare edge cases that are rarely encountered in typical usage.

Ethical hackers must adapt and refine their techniques continually, similar to artisans perfecting their craft over time.

The world of advanced artifact exploitation is dynamic, with new challenges and opportunities constantly emerging.

Ethical hackers must stay up-to-date with the latest software developments and security trends, similar to scientists exploring the frontiers of their field.

The identification and exploitation of advanced artifacts can have far-reaching implications, much like discovering hidden treasure that can change the course of history.

These artifacts may lead to critical vulnerabilities that, if left unchecked, could result in data breaches, system compromises, or other adverse consequences.

Ethical hackers who excel in this field play a crucial role in mitigating these risks by uncovering and addressing advanced artifacts before they can be exploited by malicious actors.

However, ethical considerations are paramount, and responsible disclosure of vulnerabilities is essential to ensure that software vendors can develop and deploy patches promptly.

In some cases, ethical hackers may receive recognition, rewards, or bug bounties for their efforts, akin to receiving accolades for solving a challenging puzzle.

Exploiting advanced artifacts is not only about discovering vulnerabilities but also about contributing to the improvement of software and systems.

Ethical hackers work closely with software vendors to provide technical details and assistance in developing fixes, much like experts collaborating to solve complex problems.

In summary, exploiting advanced artifacts is a sophisticated and dynamic aspect of ethical hacking, requiring a blend of technical expertise, creativity, and persistence.

Ethical hackers who excel in this field play a vital role in identifying and mitigating vulnerabilities that may otherwise go unnoticed, ultimately enhancing the security of software and systems.

Creative exploitation methods represent a fascinating aspect of ethical hacking, where imagination and unconventional thinking play a pivotal role.

These methods involve devising unique approaches to uncover and exploit vulnerabilities that may not be apparent through traditional means.

In the world of ethical hacking, creativity is akin to an artist's canvas, where every exploit is a potential masterpiece waiting to be crafted.

Creative hackers approach their work with an open mind, much like explorers venturing into uncharted territories in search of hidden treasures.

They understand that vulnerabilities often hide in unexpected places, and they're willing to embrace unconventional ideas to find them.

Creative exploitation methods encompass a wide range of techniques, from unconventional data inputs to novel combinations of vulnerabilities.

Hackers in this category may experiment with data payloads, injecting unusual characters or patterns that trigger unexpected behaviors in the target system.

To succeed in creative exploitation, ethical hackers must think outside the box, much like inventors who come up with groundbreaking solutions to complex problems.

They may combine seemingly unrelated vulnerabilities, exploiting one to bypass protections in another, creating a unique path to compromise.

Sometimes, creative hackers even repurpose legitimate features of software or systems, using them in unintended ways to gain unauthorized access.

This approach is akin to using everyday objects as tools in an unexpected and imaginative manner.

Creative hackers often share a common trait with storytellers: they create narratives or scenarios that guide their exploitation attempts.

They envision how vulnerabilities could be chained together to form a compelling story of compromise, much like a writer crafting a thrilling plot.

The exploitation process becomes an adventure, with each step in the attack chain contributing to the unfolding story.

Creative exploitation methods require not only technical skills but also an understanding of human psychology and system behaviors.

Hackers in this category may leverage social engineering techniques to manipulate users or employees into unwittingly assisting in their exploits.

This psychological aspect adds depth to their creative approach, making their attacks more sophisticated and effective.

To excel in creative exploitation, ethical hackers often draw inspiration from diverse sources, much like artists who gather ideas from various cultures and disciplines.

They may study unrelated fields, such as psychology, game theory, or even art, to find new perspectives that inform their hacking strategies.

Creativity also plays a significant role in finding zero-day vulnerabilities, which are previously unknown flaws that have not been patched.

Creative hackers may invest time in analyzing software or systems in unique ways, uncovering vulnerabilities that no one else has discovered.

This pioneering spirit is akin to explorers who venture into unexplored territories, charting new paths for others to follow.

The creative process in exploitation is not linear; it's more like a meandering journey filled with experimentation and discovery.

Hackers often encounter dead ends, but these setbacks are opportunities to learn and adapt, much like inventors refining their prototypes.

Creative hackers understand that their work has real-world consequences, and they prioritize responsible disclosure to protect users and organizations.

They collaborate with software vendors to ensure that vulnerabilities are addressed promptly, much like conscientious researchers sharing their findings for the greater good.

In summary, creative exploitation methods showcase the artistry and ingenuity of ethical hacking.

These hackers approach their craft with open minds, embracing unconventional ideas and unconventional paths to uncover and exploit vulnerabilities.

Their work is not just about finding flaws; it's about creating unique and compelling narratives of compromise, ultimately contributing to the improvement of software and systems security.

Chapter 4: Advanced Web Application Security Testing

Real-world web application exploits provide valuable insights into the vulnerabilities and attack techniques that malicious actors commonly use to compromise web applications.

Studying these exploits is essential for both security professionals and developers to understand the evolving threat landscape.

Web applications are a prime target for cybercriminals because they often process sensitive data and perform critical functions.

Exploiting vulnerabilities in web applications can lead to data breaches, financial losses, and reputational damage.

One of the most prevalent web application vulnerabilities is SQL injection (SQLi), which allows attackers to manipulate an application's database queries.

In real-world exploits, attackers craft malicious SQL queries to extract, modify, or delete sensitive data stored in the database.

SQL injection attacks can be devastating, as they can lead to the exposure of user credentials, financial records, and other confidential information.

Cross-site scripting (XSS) is another widespread vulnerability where attackers inject malicious scripts into web pages viewed by other users.

Real-world XSS exploits often target session cookies, enabling attackers to hijack user sessions and impersonate legitimate users.

These exploits can lead to unauthorized access, data theft, and the injection of harmful content into web applications.

Security misconfigurations are a common source of real-world web application vulnerabilities.

Attackers seek out improperly configured security settings that expose sensitive information or grant unauthorized access.

In some cases, developers inadvertently expose sensitive files or directories, allowing attackers to view and download confidential data.

Exploits targeting security misconfigurations can lead to data leaks and unauthorized access to critical systems.

Another prevalent threat is remote code execution (RCE), where attackers execute malicious code on a web server or application.

Real-world RCE exploits can lead to complete compromise of the application, allowing attackers to take control of the server and execute arbitrary commands.

Such attacks can result in data breaches, service disruptions, and significant security incidents.

File upload vulnerabilities are frequently exploited to upload malicious files to web applications.

Attackers may abuse these vulnerabilities to deliver malware, deface websites, or compromise server integrity.

Real-world file upload exploits often involve bypassing file type restrictions and executing malicious code on the server.

Cross-Site Request Forgery (CSRF) is a type of exploit where attackers trick users into performing actions without their consent.

Real-world CSRF exploits can lead to unauthorized changes in user account settings, such as password changes or account deletion.

Phishing attacks often incorporate CSRF techniques to deceive users into taking actions that benefit the attacker.

Broken authentication and session management vulnerabilities are prime targets for attackers seeking to gain unauthorized access to web applications.

Real-world exploits of these vulnerabilities involve session fixation, session hijacking, and brute force attacks on login credentials.

Successful attacks can result in account takeovers and unauthorized access to sensitive data.

To protect against real-world web application exploits, security professionals and developers must prioritize security from the initial design phase.

This includes conducting regular security assessments, such as penetration testing and code reviews, to identify and remediate vulnerabilities.

Web application firewalls (WAFs) can help mitigate common exploits by filtering and blocking malicious traffic.

Implementing strong access controls, proper input validation, and secure coding practices can also reduce the risk of real-world exploits.

Additionally, keeping web application frameworks and libraries up-to-date is crucial to address known vulnerabilities.

User education and awareness training can help mitigate attacks that rely on social engineering techniques.

In summary, understanding real-world web application exploits is essential for securing web applications effectively.

These exploits demonstrate the real threats that web applications face, from SQL injection and XSS to security misconfigurations and file upload vulnerabilities.

By adopting a proactive security approach, organizations can defend against these exploits and protect their web applications and users from harm.

Cloud security presents unique challenges and opportunities as organizations increasingly rely on cloud computing to drive innovation and scalability in their operations.

One of the key challenges in cloud security is the shared responsibility model, which delineates the responsibilities of cloud service providers and customers.

While cloud providers are responsible for securing the infrastructure, customers are responsible for securing their applications and data.

This division of responsibility requires organizations to implement robust security practices to protect their assets in the cloud.

Another challenge is the dynamic nature of cloud environments, which can make it challenging to maintain visibility and control over assets and configurations.

The ephemeral nature of cloud resources can lead to forgotten or unmonitored assets, creating potential security blind spots.

Organizations need to adopt automated monitoring and security solutions to address this challenge effectively.

Data security and privacy are paramount concerns in the cloud, particularly when data is stored or processed across various regions and jurisdictions.

Data encryption, access controls, and compliance with data protection regulations are crucial for addressing these concerns.

In multi-cloud or hybrid cloud environments, the complexity of managing security across different platforms and providers can be overwhelming.

Consistent security policies and centralized management tools can help streamline security operations.

Identity and access management (IAM) is a critical aspect of cloud security, as unauthorized access can lead to data breaches and system compromises.

Implementing strong authentication, role-based access controls, and least privilege principles is essential to mitigating this risk.

The use of containers and serverless computing introduces additional security considerations in cloud environments.

Vulnerabilities in container images or serverless functions can be exploited by attackers, emphasizing the need for secure development practices and vulnerability scanning.

Cloud misconfigurations are a common source of security incidents in the cloud.

Organizations must perform regular security assessments to identify and remediate misconfigurations, such as overly permissive access policies or exposed resources.

Threat detection and incident response are critical components of cloud security.

Real-time monitoring and automated alerting can help organizations detect and respond to security incidents promptly.

Implementing a well-defined incident response plan ensures that incidents are handled effectively to minimize damage.

The adoption of DevOps and continuous integration/continuous deployment (CI/CD) practices has transformed the way software is developed and deployed in the cloud.

Security must be integrated into the DevOps pipeline to ensure that vulnerabilities are detected and addressed early in the development process.

Security automation and orchestration tools can help integrate security into CI/CD pipelines seamlessly. The cloud-native landscape offers a wide range of security solutions and services that organizations can leverage to enhance their cloud security posture. These include cloud security posture management (CSPM) tools, cloud workload protection platforms (CWPP), and cloud access security brokers (CASB).

Organizations should evaluate and implement these solutions based on their specific security requirements.

Compliance with industry regulations and standards is essential for organizations operating in the cloud.

Cloud providers offer compliance certifications for various regulatory frameworks, but customers must also ensure that their configurations and practices align with these requirements.

Security awareness and training are vital components of a robust cloud security strategy.

Employees and stakeholders must be educated about security best practices and potential threats.

Cloud security is not a one-time effort but an ongoing process.

Regular security assessments, penetration testing, and vulnerability scanning are necessary to identify and address new security risks.

Cloud providers continuously update their services and security features.

Organizations should stay informed about these updates and take advantage of new security enhancements.

In summary, cloud security presents both challenges and opportunities for organizations.

The shared responsibility model, dynamic environments, data privacy concerns, and the need for consistent security policies all require careful consideration.

By implementing robust security practices, leveraging cloud-native security solutions, and staying vigilant, organizations can effectively protect their assets and data in the cloud.

Chapter 5: Advanced Network and Cloud Vulnerability Assessment

Cloud computing has revolutionized the way businesses operate, offering scalability, flexibility, and cost-efficiency, but it has also introduced a unique set of security challenges that must be addressed to ensure the safety of data and resources.

One of the foremost challenges in cloud security is the shared responsibility model, where cloud providers are responsible for securing the underlying infrastructure, but customers are responsible for securing their applications, data, and configurations.

This model necessitates a clear understanding of the division of responsibilities to prevent security gaps and overlaps.

Cloud providers offer a wide range of security tools and features, but it is ultimately the customer's responsibility to configure and use these resources effectively.

Data security is a top concern for organizations, particularly when data is stored, processed, or transmitted in the cloud.

Encryption, both in transit and at rest, is a fundamental security measure to protect sensitive information from unauthorized access.

Access controls and strong authentication mechanisms are equally critical to prevent data breaches.

Managing and controlling access to cloud resources and data is challenging, especially in multi-cloud or hybrid environments.

Identity and access management (IAM) solutions help organizations enforce access policies, roles, and permissions consistently across different cloud services and platforms.

Monitoring and auditing are essential components of cloud security to detect and respond to security incidents in real-time.

Automated monitoring tools can provide insights into activities, configurations, and potential threats, allowing for timely responses and mitigation.

The dynamic nature of cloud environments, with resources being created and decommissioned rapidly, makes visibility and control a challenge.

Cloud security posture management (CSPM) tools help organizations maintain a comprehensive view of their cloud assets and configurations, identifying vulnerabilities and misconfigurations.

Security misconfigurations are a common source of cloud security incidents.

Automated checks and continuous assessment of cloud configurations help prevent misconfigurations that could expose resources to attacks.

Containers and serverless computing are integral to modern cloud applications, but they introduce unique security considerations.

Vulnerabilities in container images and serverless functions can be exploited by attackers, emphasizing the importance of secure development practices, code reviews, and vulnerability scanning.

Multi-cloud or hybrid cloud environments increase complexity but also provide redundancy and flexibility.

However, consistent security policies and centralized management tools are necessary to ensure that security is not compromised across different cloud providers.

Compliance with industry-specific regulations and standards remains a critical concern for organizations, and cloud providers offer certifications and compliance tools to help customers align with these requirements. Cloud access security brokers (CASBs) are increasingly valuable in cloud security by providing visibility and control over cloud usage, data protection, and compliance. DevOps and continuous integration/continuous deployment (CI/CD) practices have become standard in cloud-native development, but they also require integrating security seamlessly into the development pipeline. DevSecOps emphasizes the importance of incorporating security checks and automated testing into the CI/CD process to identify and remediate vulnerabilities early in the development cycle. Incident response planning is crucial for effective cloud security. Organizations should have well-defined incident response plans, outlining procedures for detecting, reporting, and mitigating security incidents in the cloud. Security awareness and training are essential to empower employees and stakeholders to recognize and respond to security threats effectively.

Regular security assessments, penetration testing, and vulnerability scanning are necessary to identify and address emerging security risks and threats.

Cloud providers continuously improve their security features, and organizations should stay informed about updates and enhancements to leverage the latest security capabilities.

In summary, cloud security is a dynamic and evolving field, and addressing its challenges requires a comprehensive and proactive approach.

By understanding the shared responsibility model, implementing strong access controls, encryption, and monitoring, and leveraging the tools and services provided by cloud providers, organizations can strengthen their cloud security posture and protect their data and resources effectively. In the ever-evolving landscape of cybersecurity, advanced network vulnerability assessment strategies play a crucial role in safeguarding organizations from potential threats and vulnerabilities.

These strategies go beyond traditional vulnerability scanning and delve into comprehensive assessments that encompass the entire network infrastructure.

Advanced network vulnerability assessment involves a proactive and systematic approach to identifying weaknesses and security gaps in an organization's network. It aims to provide a holistic view of the network's security posture, enabling organizations to mitigate vulnerabilities before they can be exploited by malicious actors. One fundamental aspect of advanced network vulnerability assessment is the use of both automated and manual testing methods. Automated vulnerability scanning tools are valuable for quickly identifying known vulnerabilities and common misconfigurations in the network. These tools can scan a large number of assets and provide a baseline assessment of security. However, automated tools have limitations, as they may not detect certain vulnerabilities that require more sophisticated testing techniques. Manual testing, on the other hand, involves the expertise of skilled security professionals who can identify vulnerabilities that automated tools may miss. This includes logic flaws, business logic vulnerabilities, and complex configuration issues that are often beyond the scope of automated scans. Advanced network vulnerability assessments often begin with a thorough reconnaissance phase, where security professionals gather information about the organization's network infrastructure, systems, and applications.

This information includes network diagrams, IP addresses, domain names, and details about the organization's internet presence.

Reconnaissance is essential for understanding the attack surface and identifying potential entry points for attackers. Once the reconnaissance phase is complete, the next step is to perform a vulnerability assessment by scanning the network for known vulnerabilities.

This involves using automated scanning tools to identify common weaknesses, such as outdated software, missing security patches, and misconfigured settings.

The results of these scans provide a baseline assessment of the network's security posture.

However, it is crucial to remember that automated scans alone are not sufficient for advanced network vulnerability assessment. To uncover more complex vulnerabilities, security professionals must conduct manual testing and analysis. One effective technique used in advanced vulnerability assessment is penetration testing, where ethical hackers simulate real-world attacks to identify vulnerabilities that automated scans might miss. Penetration testers use various tools and techniques to exploit vulnerabilities and gain unauthorized access to systems.

This process helps organizations understand the potential impact of security weaknesses and provides valuable insights into how to remediate them.

Another critical aspect of advanced network vulnerability assessment is the assessment of security controls and configurations.

This involves reviewing firewall rules, access control lists, intrusion detection and prevention system (IDPS) configurations, and other security measures to ensure they are properly configured and effectively protecting the network.

Misconfigured security controls can create significant vulnerabilities, as they may allow unauthorized access or fail to detect and block malicious activity.

In addition to automated scanning and manual testing, advanced vulnerability assessment strategies also involve analyzing the results of security monitoring and incident response data.

Security professionals review logs and alerts to identify patterns of suspicious activity and potential indicators of compromise.

This proactive approach can help organizations detect and respond to security threats before they escalate.

Furthermore, advanced network vulnerability assessment includes the assessment of third-party and supply chain risks.

Organizations often rely on third-party vendors and suppliers for various services and products, which can introduce security vulnerabilities into their networks.

Assessing the security posture of third-party vendors and their products is crucial to ensure that they do not pose a threat to the organization's network.

In today's interconnected world, advanced network vulnerability assessment strategies must also consider the impact of cloud computing and virtualization on an organization's security posture.

Cloud environments introduce unique security challenges, as organizations may have limited visibility and control over their cloud infrastructure.

Advanced assessment strategies should include the evaluation of cloud security controls and configurations to ensure the integrity and confidentiality of data stored in the cloud.

Moreover, organizations should consider the impact of containerization and microservices architecture on their network security.

Containerized applications and microservices can introduce additional complexities and potential vulnerabilities that require thorough assessment.

In summary, advanced network vulnerability assessment strategies are essential for organizations seeking to protect their network infrastructure from evolving threats and vulnerabilities.

These strategies combine automated scanning, manual testing, security control assessment, incident response analysis, third-party risk assessment, and consideration of cloud and containerization technologies to provide a comprehensive view of the network's security posture.

By adopting advanced assessment techniques and proactively addressing vulnerabilities, organizations can enhance their overall cybersecurity and reduce the risk of security incidents.

Chapter 6: Reverse Engineering and Malware Analysis

Reverse engineering is a valuable skill in the world of cybersecurity and software development.

It involves the process of deconstructing a software program, hardware device, or system to understand its inner workings, functionality, and design.

Reverse engineering is not only used for analyzing and understanding proprietary software but also for identifying security vulnerabilities, improving software compatibility, and creating interoperable solutions.

In practice, reverse engineering often begins with the examination of a compiled binary or executable file.

These files contain machine code that is not human-readable, making it challenging to understand the program's logic and functionality.

To make sense of the binary code, reverse engineers use disassemblers and decompilers.

Disassemblers convert the binary code into assembly language, which is a lower-level representation of the code that is somewhat more human-readable.

Decompilers, on the other hand, attempt to reconstruct higher-level source code from the binary.

Both tools are essential for reverse engineers to gain insights into how a program works.

Reverse engineers also rely on debugging tools and techniques to step through the code and observe its behavior in real-time.

This allows them to identify specific functions, variables, and data structures within the program.

Furthermore, reverse engineers often use dynamic analysis to monitor the program's runtime behavior and interactions with the operating system and other components.

This approach can reveal how the program communicates with external resources, processes data, and responds to various inputs.

In addition to examining compiled code, reverse engineers may analyze data files and network traffic associated with a software application.

This can help uncover file formats, data structures, and communication protocols used by the program.

For example, reverse engineers may reverse engineer file formats to create custom tools for extracting and manipulating data from proprietary file types.

Network traffic analysis can reveal how a program communicates with remote servers and services, which is crucial for understanding its functionality and identifying potential security issues.

Reverse engineering is not limited to software; it also applies to hardware devices and systems.

Embedded systems, such as IoT devices and firmware-based appliances, often require reverse engineering to understand their operation fully.

Hardware reverse engineering involves analyzing the physical components of a device, such as circuit boards, chips, and connectors.

Reverse engineers may use tools like logic analyzers and oscilloscopes to capture and analyze electrical signals, helping them understand how hardware components interact.

One common goal of reverse engineering is to identify vulnerabilities and security weaknesses in software and hardware.

Reverse engineers actively look for security flaws that could be exploited by malicious actors.

This may include identifying buffer overflows, injection vulnerabilities, privilege escalation flaws, and cryptographic weaknesses.

Once vulnerabilities are identified, security researchers can responsibly disclose them to the software or hardware vendor for remediation.

Reverse engineering is also used for software interoperability and compatibility.

When working with legacy software or proprietary file formats, reverse engineers can develop custom solutions to make data and software more accessible.

For example, reverse engineering might be used to create compatibility layers or converters that allow old software to run on modern operating systems or enable the use of file formats that were previously unsupported.

Reverse engineering can also be employed to create patches or modifications for software.

These modifications can be used to enhance software functionality, remove restrictions, or extend the lifespan of legacy applications.

However, it's important to note that modifying software without proper authorization may infringe on intellectual property rights or violate software licensing agreements.

Therefore, reverse engineers must be mindful of legal and ethical considerations when creating software modifications.

Reverse engineering is not only a technical skill but also a creative and problem-solving endeavor.

It requires a deep understanding of computer science, programming languages, and low-level systems.

It also demands patience, attention to detail, and the ability to think critically and analytically.

Reverse engineers often collaborate with others, sharing insights, tools, and techniques within the cybersecurity and software development communities.

Furthermore, reverse engineering is an ever-evolving field, as new software and hardware technologies continually emerge, presenting fresh challenges and opportunities for exploration.

In summary, reverse engineering is a multifaceted practice that plays a crucial role in cybersecurity, software development, and hardware analysis.

It involves the disassembly, analysis, and understanding of software and hardware components, leading to valuable insights, vulnerability discovery, and the creation of interoperable solutions.

Reverse engineers use a combination of tools, techniques, and expertise to decode and comprehend complex systems, making it an essential skill in the modern digital landscape.

Analyzing advanced malware samples is a critical aspect of cybersecurity, as it helps security professionals understand the tactics, techniques, and procedures (TTPs) employed by malicious actors.

These TTPs can range from simple, known techniques to highly sophisticated and novel approaches designed to evade detection.

Analyzing malware samples is akin to dissecting a digital organism to uncover its inner workings and functionalities.

One common goal of malware analysis is to identify the malware's purpose, such as whether it's designed for data exfiltration, information theft, or remote control of compromised systems.

To accomplish this, analysts often start by reverse engineering the malware, which involves examining its code and behavior.

Reverse engineering is a process that aims to understand how the malware operates, including its communication with command-and-control servers, its propagation methods, and its exploitation techniques.

Malware analysts use specialized tools like disassemblers and debuggers to disassemble and inspect the binary code, making it more understandable and revealing its logic.

Behavioral analysis is another critical aspect of malware analysis, focusing on how the malware behaves when executed.

This involves running the malware in a controlled environment, typically within a sandbox or virtual machine, to observe its actions without risking harm to real systems.

During behavioral analysis, analysts monitor network traffic, file system changes, and system calls to detect any malicious activities.

The goal is to capture indicators of compromise (IOCs) that can be used to detect and prevent future infections.

Network traffic analysis is particularly important for understanding how the malware communicates with external servers or peers.

This can reveal the infrastructure used by the attackers and provide insights into their command-and-control infrastructure.

Additionally, analysts examine the malware's persistence mechanisms, which allow it to maintain a foothold on a compromised system even after a reboot.

This may involve registry modifications, service creation, or other techniques that ensure the malware runs at system startup.

Beyond understanding the malware's basic functionality, analysts also seek to uncover any evasion techniques employed by the malware.

Advanced malware often employs anti-analysis and anti-debugging tricks to thwart researchers' efforts.

These tricks can include checks for the presence of debugging tools, sandbox environments, or virtual machines, and attempts to evade detection.

Malware authors may use polymorphic or metamorphic code to obfuscate the malware, making it harder to detect and analyze.

Additionally, rootkit techniques may be employed to hide the malware's presence on an infected system.

To overcome these challenges, malware analysts need to employ various anti-evasion techniques and utilize advanced tools to bypass these countermeasures.

Another important aspect of malware analysis is the identification of vulnerabilities that the malware exploits.

This information can be crucial for organizations to patch or mitigate vulnerabilities in their systems.

For example, if the malware exploits a known vulnerability in a particular software component, organizations can prioritize patching that vulnerability to prevent future attacks.

Malware analysis also involves examining the malware's code for signs of sophistication, including complex algorithms, encryption techniques, or the use of zero-day vulnerabilities.

Advanced malware often employs these tactics to make analysis and detection more challenging.

Furthermore, malware analysts may use sandboxing environments with specific configurations to test the malware's behavior under different conditions.

By doing so, they can better understand how the malware adapts and evolves in response to various environmental factors.

Moreover, analyzing malware samples requires continuous learning and staying updated on the latest threats and techniques employed by malicious actors.

Cybersecurity professionals often share their findings and insights within the community to collaborate and enhance their collective knowledge.

In summary, analyzing advanced malware samples is a complex and ever-evolving field in cybersecurity.

It involves reverse engineering, behavioral analysis, and evasion technique detection to uncover the malware's functionality, tactics, and vulnerabilities it exploits.

Cybersecurity professionals must employ a combination of tools, techniques, and expertise to effectively dissect and understand these digital threats, contributing to the ongoing effort to protect digital environments from cyberattacks.

Chapter 7: Evasive Techniques and Advanced CTF Challenges

Advanced Capture The Flag (CTF) challenges are an exciting and essential part of cybersecurity education and training, pushing participants to apply their skills in solving complex and real-world problems.

These challenges go beyond the basics and require a deep understanding of various cybersecurity domains, making them suitable for experienced professionals and enthusiasts seeking to hone their expertise.

CTF challenges often simulate real-world scenarios, providing participants with opportunities to practice and develop their skills in a controlled environment.

In advanced CTFs, participants face a wide range of challenges that encompass cryptography, reverse engineering, web application security, binary exploitation, and more.

One of the distinguishing features of advanced CTF challenges is the complexity of the problems presented, which demand a high level of problem-solving and critical thinking.

Participants must think creatively, apply multiple techniques, and often collaborate with teammates to solve these intricate puzzles.

Cryptography challenges in advanced CTFs require participants to decrypt, encrypt, or analyze cryptographic protocols and algorithms.

These challenges may involve breaking encryption schemes, deciphering encoded messages, or finding weaknesses in cryptographic implementations.

To succeed in cryptography challenges, participants need a strong foundation in cryptography principles and a knack for recognizing patterns and vulnerabilities in cryptographic systems.

Reverse engineering challenges are another common category in advanced CTFs, where participants are tasked with deconstructing and understanding the inner workings of software or hardware.

Reverse engineering often involves disassembling binaries, analyzing code, and identifying vulnerabilities or backdoors hidden within the software.

These challenges test participants' ability to read and interpret assembly language, follow program flow, and identify vulnerabilities or malicious functionality.

Web application security challenges in advanced CTFs focus on finding and exploiting vulnerabilities in web applications.

Participants may need to uncover vulnerabilities like SQL injection, Cross-Site Scripting (XSS), Cross-Site Request Forgery (CSRF), or insecure authentication mechanisms in web applications.

Solving web application security challenges requires a deep understanding of web technologies, web application architecture, and common security flaws.

Binary exploitation challenges in advanced CTFs are designed to test participants' skills in exploiting software vulnerabilities.

These challenges often involve finding and exploiting buffer overflows, format string vulnerabilities, or other memory corruption issues in vulnerable binaries.

Participants need expertise in programming languages, memory management, and assembly language to excel in binary exploitation challenges.

Advanced CTFs also include challenges related to forensics and network analysis, where participants investigate incidents, analyze network traffic, and recover hidden information from digital artifacts.

These challenges mimic real-world scenarios faced by cybersecurity professionals when responding to security incidents.

Solving forensics and network analysis challenges requires knowledge of digital forensics tools and techniques, as well as an understanding of network protocols and packet analysis.

Pwnables challenges are another subset of advanced CTFs that involve exploiting vulnerabilities in custom-made programs or services.

Participants often need to gain control over a remote system or service by exploiting vulnerabilities in the provided binaries.

These challenges demand a deep understanding of software exploitation techniques and low-level system interactions.

In advanced CTFs, participants often encounter "puzzle" challenges that require a combination of technical skills and lateral thinking.

These puzzles may involve cryptography, steganography, or other forms of data manipulation.

Participants must decipher hidden messages, extract meaningful information from seemingly innocuous data, or identify patterns that lead to the solution.

One of the unique aspects of advanced CTF challenges is the "capture the flag" element, where participants aim to find hidden flags or tokens that prove they have successfully solved a challenge.

Flags are typically strings of text or codes hidden within the challenge's environment, and participants must submit these flags to earn points.

The competitive nature of CTFs adds excitement and motivation for participants to tackle increasingly difficult challenges.

To succeed in advanced CTFs, participants often form teams to leverage their collective expertise and skills.

Teamwork allows members to pool their knowledge and collaborate on solving challenges more efficiently.

In addition to technical skills, effective communication and coordination within a team are essential for success in advanced CTF competitions.

Advanced CTF challenges not only offer an opportunity to test and expand one's technical skills but also provide exposure to cutting-edge cybersecurity concepts and techniques.

Many challenges are inspired by real-world vulnerabilities and incidents, making them a valuable training ground for cybersecurity professionals.

Participation in advanced CTFs can also lead to networking opportunities and recognition within the cybersecurity community, as top-performing teams and individuals are often celebrated.

Furthermore, CTFs provide a platform for cybersecurity enthusiasts to stay updated on the latest security trends, tools, and vulnerabilities.

In summary, advanced Capture The Flag (CTF) challenges are a captivating and invaluable aspect of cybersecurity education and training.

These challenges require participants to delve into complex and diverse cybersecurity domains, from cryptography and reverse engineering to web application security and binary exploitation.

By tackling advanced CTF challenges, participants hone their technical skills, critical thinking, and problem-solving abilities, making them better prepared to defend against real-world cyber threats. Evasion techniques and countermeasures play a critical role in the ever-evolving landscape of cybersecurity.

As cyber threats become increasingly sophisticated, the need to understand evasion tactics and how to defend against them has never been more important.

Evasion techniques refer to the methods used by attackers to avoid detection and bypass security measures, allowing them to carry out malicious activities undetected.

These techniques can encompass a wide range of tactics, from concealing malware to disguising malicious network traffic.

One of the most common evasion techniques employed by attackers is the use of encryption to obfuscate malicious payloads and communication.

By encrypting their communications, attackers can make it challenging for security tools to inspect and identify malicious content.

Countermeasures against encryption-based evasion techniques include the use of advanced inspection methods that can decrypt and inspect encrypted traffic for threats.

Attackers also frequently use polymorphic malware, which constantly changes its code and appearance to evade detection by antivirus software.

Polymorphic malware presents a significant challenge to traditional signature-based detection methods, as the malware's code appears different each time it is executed.

To counter polymorphic malware, security solutions employ behavior-based detection, heuristics, and machine learning algorithms to identify malicious behavior patterns. Another evasion technique is the use of steganography, where attackers hide malicious code or data within innocent-looking files, such as images or documents. Steganography can be challenging to detect, as the malicious payload is concealed within legitimate-looking content. Countermeasures for steganography involve the use of specialized tools and techniques to analyze files for hidden content and anomalies.

Attackers may also use techniques like code obfuscation to make it difficult for security analysts to understand and reverse engineer malicious code.

Obfuscated code can be challenging to decipher, slowing down the process of identifying and mitigating threats.

Security professionals employ various deobfuscation and code analysis techniques to reveal the true nature of obfuscated code.

To evade network-based intrusion detection systems (IDS) and intrusion prevention systems (IPS), attackers may fragment packets or use tunneling protocols to disguise their activities.

Fragmented or tunneled traffic can bypass security controls that rely on analyzing packet headers and content. Countermeasures include configuring IDS/IPS systems to reassemble fragmented packets before inspection and monitoring for known tunneling protocols.

Evasion techniques can also be applied to phishing emails, where attackers use social engineering tactics to deceive recipients. These emails may contain malicious attachments or links that lead to compromised websites.

To defend against phishing attacks, user education and awareness programs are crucial, as well as email filtering solutions that can identify and quarantine phishing emails. Attackers frequently employ zero-day vulnerabilities to carry out their attacks, taking advantage of unpatched software flaws for which no security patches are available.

To counter zero-day attacks, organizations must prioritize patch management and adopt security solutions that offer real-time threat detection and prevention.

Another evasion technique involves blending malicious traffic with legitimate network traffic to avoid detection by intrusion detection systems. This can be achieved by mimicking the behavior of legitimate applications and users, making it challenging for security tools to distinguish between genuine and malicious traffic. Countermeasures include anomaly detection and behavior analysis to identify deviations from normal network behavior. Evasion techniques extend to evasion of endpoint security solutions, where attackers aim to avoid detection by antivirus software and endpoint detection and response (EDR) solutions.

Attackers may employ fileless malware, which resides only in memory and leaves no traces on disk, making it difficult to detect.

Countermeasures involve leveraging endpoint security solutions that can monitor and analyze the behavior of running processes and memory for signs of malicious activity.

Evasion techniques are not limited to malware-based attacks but can also be used in various stages of the cyberattack lifecycle, including reconnaissance and lateral movement. Attackers may use techniques like IP spoofing to hide their true IP addresses during reconnaissance activities, making it challenging for defenders to trace the source of the attack.

To counter IP spoofing, network filtering and monitoring solutions can be employed to detect and block suspicious traffic.

Evasion techniques are continually evolving as attackers seek new ways to bypass security measures.

To stay ahead of these threats, organizations must adopt a proactive and multi-layered security strategy that combines the use of advanced security tools, employee training, and ongoing threat intelligence.

Collaboration within the cybersecurity community is also crucial for sharing knowledge and developing effective countermeasures against emerging evasion techniques.

In summary, evasion techniques are a persistent challenge in the field of cybersecurity, as attackers constantly seek new methods to avoid detection and carry out malicious activities.

Understanding these techniques and implementing effective countermeasures is essential for organizations to protect their digital assets and data from evolving threats.

Chapter 8: Bug Bounty Program Maximization Strategies

Maximizing bug bounty rewards is a goal for every bug hunter who participates in bug bounty programs. Earning substantial rewards not only provides recognition but also helps bug hunters to make a living from their skills and expertise.

To maximize bug bounty rewards, bug hunters need to follow a strategic approach that involves various aspects of their bug hunting activities.

First and foremost, bug hunters should focus on targeting high-value vulnerabilities.

Bug bounty programs typically assign different bounties based on the severity of the vulnerabilities discovered. Focusing on critical and high-severity vulnerabilities can lead to more substantial rewards. However, finding such vulnerabilities can be more challenging, requiring advanced skills and extensive testing. Bug hunters should also keep an eye on the latest trends and technologies. As technology evolves, new types of vulnerabilities emerge, and companies often introduce new products or features that may contain security flaws.

Staying up to date with these developments can give bug hunters an edge in discovering novel vulnerabilities.

Moreover, actively participating in bug bounty programs from multiple organizations can increase the chances of finding lucrative bugs.

Different organizations have different security postures and technologies, which can lead to a wider range of vulnerabilities to discover.

Engaging with the security community is another crucial aspect of maximizing bug bounty rewards.

Bug hunters can learn from their peers, share insights, and collaborate on research projects, leading to a better understanding of attack vectors and exploitation techniques.

Moreover, participating in Capture The Flag (CTF) competitions and other hacking challenges can help bug hunters sharpen their skills and gain recognition within the community.

Additionally, bug hunters should build a reputation within the bug bounty community by consistently submitting high-quality reports and cooperating with program owners.

A strong reputation can lead to invitations to private bug bounty programs, which often offer higher rewards.

In the bug hunting process, it's essential to maintain proper documentation.

Keeping detailed records of the vulnerabilities discovered, including proof of concept (PoC) code and clear explanations, can facilitate the reporting process and increase the chances of receiving a higher bounty.

Furthermore, maintaining professionalism and good communication skills when reporting vulnerabilities is crucial.

Clear and concise vulnerability reports that provide all the necessary information can expedite the resolution process and enhance the chances of a higher payout.

Program owners appreciate bug hunters who make their job easier by providing well-documented reports.

Bug hunters should also be patient and persistent.

Not every bug report will lead to a substantial reward, and sometimes it may take time to build a rapport with program owners.

Persistence in hunting for vulnerabilities and consistently submitting reports can eventually lead to more significant payouts.

In some cases, program owners may offer bonuses or increase bounties for bug hunters who consistently provide valuable contributions to their security efforts.

Networking within the bug hunting community can also open up opportunities for collaboration and mentorship.

Experienced bug hunters may be willing to share their knowledge and provide guidance to newcomers, helping them improve their skills and find higher-paying bugs.

Moreover, bug hunters should consider diversifying their bug hunting activities.

While web application vulnerabilities are prevalent, exploring other areas such as mobile apps, IoT devices, and network infrastructure can lead to the discovery of unique and valuable vulnerabilities.

Diversification can also help bug hunters avoid burnout by providing fresh challenges and opportunities.

Maintaining a disciplined bug hunting schedule is essential.

Bug hunting requires consistent effort and dedication.

Establishing a routine for bug hunting activities, setting goals, and managing time effectively can lead to a more productive bug hunting experience.

Moreover, bug hunters should continuously improve their technical skills.

Security is an ever-evolving field, and staying updated with the latest tools, techniques, and vulnerabilities is essential.

By investing in skill development, bug hunters can increase their chances of finding more critical bugs and earning higher rewards.

Being ethical and responsible is a fundamental principle of bug hunting.

Bug hunters should always adhere to the terms and conditions of bug bounty programs and respect the privacy and security of the organizations they test.

Unethical behavior, such as unauthorized access or data breaches, can lead to legal consequences and damage one's reputation in the bug hunting community.

Additionally, bug hunters should prioritize the disclosure of vulnerabilities to program owners.

Responsible disclosure ensures that organizations have the opportunity to fix vulnerabilities before they can be exploited by malicious actors.

Lastly, bug hunters should consider the financial aspects of bug hunting.

Understanding the tax implications of bug bounty rewards, setting financial goals, and managing income effectively can help bug hunters maximize the benefits of their bug hunting efforts.

In summary, maximizing bug bounty rewards requires a multifaceted approach that encompasses technical skills, professionalism, networking, and a commitment to ethical behavior.

Bug hunters who follow a strategic approach, continuously improve their skills, and maintain a strong reputation within the bug hunting community are more likely to achieve their goal of earning substantial bug bounty rewards.

Negotiation plays a crucial role in bug bounty hunting, as it can significantly impact the outcome and rewards of a bug hunting engagement.

Bug hunters often find themselves negotiating with program owners over the severity and impact of vulnerabilities they've discovered.

Successful negotiation requires a combination of technical expertise, effective communication, and strategic thinking.

When negotiating with program owners, bug hunters should provide clear and detailed information about the vulnerabilities they've found.

This includes a thorough explanation of the vulnerability's impact on the target system or application, along with evidence such as proof-of-concept (PoC) code or screenshots.

Providing this information upfront can help program owners understand the severity of the issue and the potential risk it poses.

Bug hunters should also be prepared to answer any questions or concerns raised by program owners.

This may involve explaining the technical details of the vulnerability, the likelihood of exploitation, and the potential consequences if left unpatched.

Effective communication is essential during negotiations, as bug hunters must convey their findings and recommendations in a clear and concise manner.

Using language that program owners can understand, avoiding technical jargon, and focusing on the business impact of the vulnerability can help facilitate productive discussions.

In some cases, program owners may initially underestimate the severity of a vulnerability or offer a lower bounty than the bug hunter believes is fair.

In such situations, bug hunters should be prepared to make a compelling case for the severity and impact of the vulnerability. This may involve presenting additional evidence or real-world scenarios that demonstrate the potential harm if the vulnerability were to be exploited.

Bug hunters should also be flexible in their approach to negotiations. While it's essential to advocate for fair compensation, being overly aggressive or confrontational can hinder the negotiation process.

Program owners may be more willing to cooperate and offer higher bounties if bug hunters maintain a professional and respectful tone throughout the negotiation.

Understanding the program's policies and guidelines is another critical aspect of successful negotiation.

Bug hunters should familiarize themselves with the terms and conditions of the bug bounty program, as well as any specific policies related to payouts and rewards.

This knowledge can help bug hunters navigate the negotiation process and ensure that their requests align with the program's rules.

Additionally, bug hunters should be aware of the program's budget constraints.

Some bug bounty programs have limited budgets for payouts, and program owners may need to balance their financial resources across multiple bug reports.

Being mindful of these constraints and approaching negotiations with reasonable expectations can lead to more successful outcomes.

Building a positive relationship with program owners can also be beneficial in the long run. Establishing trust and a reputation for professionalism can lead to more open and cooperative negotiations in the future.

Bug hunters who consistently provide high-quality reports, adhere to program guidelines, and maintain respectful communication are more likely to be viewed favorably by program owners.

Ultimately, the goal of negotiation in bug bounty hunting is to reach a mutually agreeable resolution that fairly compensates bug hunters for their efforts and the value of the vulnerabilities they've discovered.

By following best practices in negotiation, bug hunters can increase their chances of receiving fair rewards and contribute to the overall success of bug bounty programs.

Chapter 9: Legal and Ethical Considerations for Virtuosos

Navigating the legal landscape in bug bounty hunting is a critical aspect that bug hunters must consider to ensure they operate within the bounds of the law.

The intersection of ethical hacking, vulnerability disclosure, and the legal system can be complex and challenging to navigate.

While bug bounty programs are designed to encourage the responsible disclosure of vulnerabilities, bug hunters must still be mindful of legal risks.

One of the primary legal challenges in bug bounty hunting is ensuring that bug hunters do not unintentionally cross legal boundaries when conducting their assessments.

In some jurisdictions, unauthorized access to computer systems or networks can lead to criminal charges, even if the intent is to identify and report vulnerabilities.

Bug hunters should be aware of the laws and regulations in their own jurisdiction, as well as any applicable international laws that may impact their activities.

It's essential to understand the legal definitions of terms such as "unauthorized access" and "unauthorized use" to avoid inadvertently violating the law.

Additionally, bug hunters should familiarize themselves with the specific terms and conditions of bug bounty programs, as these may outline the legal parameters within which they must operate.

Some bug bounty programs may require bug hunters to obtain explicit permission before conducting security assessments, while others may have strict rules about the types of testing that are permitted.

Bug hunters should always respect the rules set forth by the program they are participating in to avoid legal complications.

Another legal consideration in bug bounty hunting is intellectual property rights.

Bug hunters often create proof-of-concept (PoC) code or other materials to demonstrate the vulnerabilities they've discovered.

It's important to understand who owns the rights to these materials and whether they can be shared publicly.

In some cases, bug hunters may be required to transfer intellectual property rights to the program owner as part of the bug bounty agreement.

Understanding the terms of these agreements and seeking legal advice if necessary can help bug hunters avoid disputes over intellectual property.

When conducting vulnerability assessments, bug hunters should also be mindful of privacy laws and regulations.

Collecting and handling personal data as part of a security assessment can raise legal concerns, especially in jurisdictions with strict data protection laws.

Bug hunters should obtain informed consent before collecting any personal data and should only access and use data for legitimate testing purposes.

Additionally, bug hunters should take steps to ensure the confidentiality and integrity of any data they encounter during their assessments.

In some cases, bug hunters may discover vulnerabilities that have the potential to expose sensitive information.

In such situations, it's crucial to handle the information responsibly and to report it promptly to the program owner.

Failure to do so could result in legal and ethical consequences.

Navigating legal challenges also involves understanding the liability protections that may be available to bug hunters.

Some jurisdictions have enacted laws that provide legal immunity to individuals who report security vulnerabilities in good faith.

These laws are often referred to as "safe harbor" provisions and are designed to encourage responsible disclosure.

However, bug hunters should be aware that the scope and applicability of these laws can vary by jurisdiction.

Before engaging in bug bounty hunting, bug hunters should research whether their jurisdiction offers legal protections for vulnerability disclosure.

It's also advisable to maintain clear and accurate records of all communications and interactions with program owners and to document the responsible disclosure process.

This documentation can serve as evidence of bug hunters' good faith efforts in the event of legal disputes.

In cases where legal issues arise during bug bounty engagements, bug hunters should consider seeking legal counsel.

Legal experts with expertise in cybersecurity and vulnerability disclosure can provide guidance and representation to help bug hunters navigate the legal process.

Ultimately, bug bounty hunting can be a rewarding and valuable pursuit, but it is not without its legal challenges.

Bug hunters must remain vigilant, informed, and proactive in addressing legal considerations to ensure that their activities are conducted responsibly and within the bounds of the law.

Ethical dilemmas are not uncommon in the world of advanced bug hunting, and they can present complex challenges for bug hunters.

One of the most common ethical dilemmas bug hunters face is the question of when to disclose a discovered vulnerability.

Bug hunters are often torn between their desire to report and remediate vulnerabilities promptly and their concern that disclosing too early could potentially put users at risk.

In many cases, bug hunters must weigh the urgency of the vulnerability against the time needed for the program owner to address the issue.

Another ethical dilemma arises when bug hunters discover vulnerabilities that have the potential for significant harm or exploitation.

In such cases, bug hunters must decide whether to report the vulnerability immediately or to wait for the program owner to respond.

Reporting too quickly could lead to exploitation by malicious actors, while delaying the report could increase the risk to users.

Bug hunters must balance the desire to act responsibly with the potential consequences of their actions.

Additionally, bug hunters often encounter situations where they discover vulnerabilities that involve ethical gray areas.

For example, a vulnerability may be present in a system that is used for surveillance or other controversial purposes.

In such cases, bug hunters must consider whether their actions could inadvertently support unethical or harmful activities.

Bug hunters may also face ethical dilemmas related to the impact of their work on individuals or organizations.

For instance, the disclosure of a critical vulnerability could lead to significant financial losses for a company or even job layoffs.

Bug hunters must consider the potential collateral damage of their actions and strive to minimize harm while still fulfilling their ethical duty to report vulnerabilities.

Another ethical consideration in bug hunting is responsible disclosure.

Bug hunters should follow established guidelines for responsible disclosure, which typically involve notifying the program owner and allowing them a reasonable amount of time to address the issue before making the vulnerability public.

However, in some cases, program owners may not respond or may fail to fix the issue in a timely manner.

Bug hunters must decide whether to extend the disclosure timeline or to escalate the matter by involving a broader community or the public.

This decision can be challenging, as it may involve a trade-off between responsible disclosure and the need to protect users from potential harm.

Ethical dilemmas can also arise when bug hunters encounter vulnerabilities in products or systems that have a significant impact on public safety or critical infrastructure.

In these cases, bug hunters may feel a heightened sense of responsibility to report and remediate the vulnerabilities promptly, given the potential consequences of an exploit.

However, they must also consider the potential for misuse of the information by malicious actors.

Navigating these ethical dilemmas often requires bug hunters to exercise judgment, consider the potential consequences of their actions, and seek guidance when needed.

Ethical bug hunting is not just about finding and reporting vulnerabilities; it also involves making choices that align with a strong moral compass and a commitment to responsible disclosure.

Bug hunters should be aware of the ethical principles and guidelines established by organizations such as the Internet Bug Bounty and the disclosure policies of the programs they engage with.

Another ethical dilemma bug hunters may encounter is related to the handling of sensitive information.

During the course of their assessments, bug hunters may come across personal or confidential data.

It is their ethical responsibility to handle such information with the utmost care and respect for privacy. This may involve redacting or anonymizing sensitive data before reporting the vulnerability to the program owner.

Bug hunters must also be cautious not to disclose any sensitive information in their public disclosures. Furthermore, the issue of financial incentives in bug hunting can raise ethical questions.

While bug hunting can be financially rewarding, bug hunters must ensure that their motivations remain ethical. Accepting bounties or rewards for vulnerabilities should not compromise bug hunters' principles of responsible and ethical disclosure.

It's essential to maintain a focus on the broader goal of improving security and protecting users rather than solely pursuing financial gain.

Ultimately, ethical dilemmas in advanced bug hunting are complex and multifaceted.

Bug hunters must continually evaluate their actions and decisions in light of their ethical responsibilities, the potential consequences of their actions, and the broader impact on security and privacy.

By adhering to ethical principles and seeking guidance when faced with difficult choices, bug hunters can navigate these dilemmas responsibly and contribute to a safer digital ecosystem.

Chapter 10: The Legacy of an Elite Ethical Hacker

Creating a positive impact on cybersecurity is a mission that encompasses the collective efforts of individuals, organizations, and the broader cybersecurity community.

It begins with recognizing the ever-evolving threat landscape and understanding the critical role that cybersecurity plays in safeguarding our digital lives.

Cybersecurity is not just a technical challenge; it is a multidimensional problem that involves technology, people, processes, and policies.

To make a positive impact, individuals and organizations must adopt a proactive and holistic approach to cybersecurity.

One essential aspect of creating a positive impact on cybersecurity is education and awareness.

It is crucial to educate individuals and organizations about the latest threats, vulnerabilities, and best practices.

This knowledge empowers people to make informed decisions and take proactive steps to protect themselves and their digital assets.

Education should start early, with cybersecurity awareness programs in schools and colleges, and continue throughout one's professional career.

Additionally, organizations should invest in ongoing cybersecurity training and awareness initiatives for their employees.

Another key element in creating a positive impact on cybersecurity is the adoption of best practices and standards.

Frameworks such as the NIST Cybersecurity Framework and ISO 27001 provide guidelines for organizations to assess their cybersecurity posture and implement effective controls.

By adhering to these standards, organizations can enhance their resilience to cyber threats and reduce the risk of breaches.

Furthermore, cybersecurity is not solely the responsibility of IT professionals.

It is a shared responsibility that extends to all individuals who use digital technologies.

Creating a cybersecurity culture within an organization is essential to ensuring that security practices are ingrained in every aspect of its operations.

This includes promoting a "security-first" mindset, where security considerations are integrated into the development of products and services from the outset.

Creating a positive impact on cybersecurity also involves collaboration and information sharing.

Cybersecurity threats are not limited by geographic borders, and attackers often target multiple organizations simultaneously.

To defend against these threats effectively, organizations must collaborate with peers, industry groups, and government agencies.

Information sharing platforms and threat intelligence sharing initiatives can help organizations stay ahead of emerging threats and vulnerabilities.

Moreover, creating a positive impact on cybersecurity requires a commitment to continuous improvement.

The threat landscape is constantly evolving, with attackers developing new techniques and tactics.

Organizations must adapt and evolve their cybersecurity strategies to keep pace with these changes.

Regular security assessments, vulnerability scans, and penetration testing are essential for identifying and addressing weaknesses.

Furthermore, organizations should establish an incident response plan to effectively manage and recover from security incidents when they occur.

Another critical aspect of creating a positive impact on cybersecurity is addressing the shortage of cybersecurity professionals.

The demand for skilled cybersecurity experts far exceeds the supply, and this talent gap poses a significant challenge.

To address this gap, organizations, educational institutions, and governments must work together to promote cybersecurity as a viable and rewarding career path.

Scholarships, internships, and training programs can help individuals acquire the necessary skills and enter the field of cybersecurity.

Furthermore, diversity and inclusion efforts are essential to ensuring that the cybersecurity workforce reflects the diversity of the communities it serves.

Creating a positive impact on cybersecurity also involves staying informed about emerging technologies and trends.

As technology evolves, new security challenges and opportunities arise.

For example, the rapid adoption of cloud computing, the Internet of Things (IoT), and artificial intelligence (AI) introduces new cybersecurity considerations.

By staying informed and adapting to these changes, individuals and organizations can better protect themselves against emerging threats.

Moreover, privacy considerations are increasingly important in the cybersecurity landscape.

Data protection regulations, such as the General Data Protection Regulation (GDPR), require organizations to prioritize the privacy of individuals' data.

By implementing robust data protection measures and respecting individuals' privacy rights, organizations can enhance their cybersecurity and build trust with their customers.

Creating a positive impact on cybersecurity is not solely a technical endeavor; it also involves advocating for policy changes and regulations that promote cybersecurity.

Engaging with policymakers and advocating for strong cybersecurity measures at the national and international levels can help shape the legal and regulatory framework for cybersecurity.

Additionally, participating in public-private partnerships can foster collaboration between government agencies and the private sector to enhance cybersecurity resilience.

Ultimately, creating a positive impact on cybersecurity is an ongoing commitment that requires the collective efforts of individuals, organizations, and the broader community.

By prioritizing education, best practices, collaboration, diversity, and adaptability, we can collectively work towards a safer and more secure digital world.

It is a shared responsibility that requires vigilance, dedication, and a commitment to staying one step ahead of cyber threats.

Mentoring plays a pivotal role in shaping the future of bug hunting and the broader field of cybersecurity.

It is the process by which experienced professionals impart their knowledge, skills, and insights to guide and support newcomers in their journey.

Mentoring in bug hunting is not only about sharing technical expertise but also about instilling the right mindset and ethical values.

As bug hunting continues to evolve, the need for skilled and ethical bug hunters grows.

Experienced bug hunters have a responsibility to mentor and nurture the next generation of ethical hackers.

One of the key aspects of mentoring in bug hunting is knowledge transfer.

Experienced bug hunters possess a wealth of knowledge about various vulnerabilities, exploitation techniques, and tools.

They have encountered diverse challenges and developed effective strategies for finding and reporting bugs.

Mentors can transfer this knowledge to their mentees through hands-on training, discussions, and real world examples.

Moreover, mentoring extends beyond technical skills; it encompasses the development of soft skills and ethical principles.

Bug hunters must learn to communicate effectively, work collaboratively, and maintain integrity in their work.

Mentors can provide guidance on how to interact with bug bounty programs, report vulnerabilities responsibly, and handle ethical dilemmas.

In addition to knowledge transfer, mentoring offers a valuable support system for newcomers.

Bug hunting can be a challenging and sometimes frustrating pursuit, especially for those just starting.

Mentors provide emotional support, encouragement, and a sense of community, helping mentees navigate the ups and downs of bug hunting.

Mentoring relationships often result in strong professional networks, where mentees can seek advice, share experiences, and collaborate on bug hunting projects.

Furthermore, mentors can help mentees set clear goals and define their bug hunting career paths.

They can provide insights into the different niches within bug hunting, such as web application security, network security, or IoT security.

By helping mentees identify their strengths and interests, mentors assist in shaping their bug hunting journey.

Mentoring is a two-way street; it benefits both mentors and mentees.

For mentors, it provides an opportunity to give back to the bug hunting community and contribute to its growth.

It can be personally fulfilling to see mentees develop their skills and succeed in bug hunting.

Mentoring also allows experienced bug hunters to stay connected with emerging trends and technologies in cybersecurity.

On the other hand, for mentees, mentoring accelerates their learning curve and helps them avoid common pitfalls.

It provides them with a roadmap for skill development and career advancement.

Mentees benefit from the experiences and wisdom of their mentors, gaining insights that would take years to acquire independently.

Furthermore, mentoring can open doors to new opportunities, such as collaborations, job referrals, or participation in bug bounty programs.

Mentors often have extensive networks and can connect mentees with industry professionals and organizations.

Effective mentoring is not limited to one-on-one interactions; it can take various forms.

Group mentoring sessions, online forums, and bug hunting communities are also valuable resources for skill development and knowledge sharing.

Bug hunting platforms and organizations may host webinars, workshops, and capture-the-flag (CTF) challenges, providing mentees with opportunities to learn and grow.

Additionally, bug bounty programs often offer mentoring programs or resources to support newcomers.

As the bug hunting community continues to expand, mentorship programs are becoming more structured and accessible.

Mentors and mentees can benefit from guidelines and best practices for establishing effective mentoring relationships.

Setting clear expectations, defining goals, and maintaining open communication are essential elements of successful mentoring.

Furthermore, mentors should be approachable, patient, and willing to adapt their teaching style to the needs of their mentees.

They should encourage mentees to ask questions, explore new areas, and take ownership of their learning.

Mentees, in turn, should be proactive, motivated, and respectful of their mentors' time and expertise.

They should be receptive to feedback and willing to put in the effort required for skill development.

In summary, mentoring is a cornerstone of the bug hunting community's growth and sustainability.

It bridges the gap between experienced bug hunters and newcomers, ensuring the transfer of knowledge, skills, and ethical values.

Mentoring fosters a culture of collaboration, support, and continuous learning.

It empowers individuals to embark on rewarding bug hunting careers, contribute to cybersecurity, and make the digital world safer for all.

Conclusion

In this comprehensive book bundle, "BUG HUNTING 101: NOVICE TO VIRTUOSO" and "WEB APPLICATION SECURITY FOR ETHICAL HACKERS," we have embarked on a journey through the fascinating world of bug hunting and web application security. Across four meticulously crafted books, we have delved deep into the realms of software vulnerabilities, ethical hacking, and advanced cybersecurity techniques.

In "BOOK 1 - BUG HUNTING: A NOVICE'S GUIDE TO SOFTWARE VULNERABILITIES," we introduced novices to the fundamentals of bug hunting. We navigated through the basics of software vulnerabilities, ethical hacking, and the critical skills needed to get started on the path to becoming a bug hunter. With a strong foundation in place, readers gained a solid understanding of how to identify and report vulnerabilities effectively.

Building upon this foundation, "BOOK 2 - INTERMEDIATE BUG HUNTING TECHNIQUES: FROM NOVICE TO SKILLED HUNTER" elevated readers to the next level of bug hunting expertise. We explored more advanced techniques, including in-depth vulnerability discovery, scanning, and enumeration. Readers honed their skills, transitioning from novices to skilled hunters, ready to tackle more complex security challenges.

"BOOK 3 - ADVANCED BUG BOUNTY HUNTING: MASTERING THE ART OF CYBERSECURITY" pushed the boundaries of bug hunting further. We delved into cryptographic flaws, network intrusion, and advanced exploitation, equipping readers with the tools and knowledge needed to become masters of cybersecurity. This book not only expanded technical prowess but also emphasized strategic engagement with bug bounty programs.

Finally, in "BOOK 4 - VIRTUOSO BUG HUNTER'S HANDBOOK: SECRETS OF THE ELITE ETHICAL HACKERS," we unlocked the secrets of the elite ethical hackers. Readers discovered the mindset, techniques, and advanced artifacts used by the virtuosos in the field. This book revealed the strategies for maximizing bug bounty program participation and addressed legal and ethical considerations for those reaching the pinnacle of bug hunting excellence.

As we conclude this remarkable journey through "BUG HUNTING 101: NOVICE TO VIRTUOSO" and "WEB APPLICATION SECURITY FOR ETHICAL HACKERS," it's essential to remember that bug hunting is not just a profession; it's a commitment to making the digital world safer. Whether you're a novice embarking on your bug hunting journey or a virtuoso at the peak of your ethical hacking career, the knowledge, skills, and ethical values you've gained will continue to have a positive impact on cybersecurity.

In this fast-evolving field, staying updated, mentoring the next generation, and embracing ethical responsibility are key to making a lasting contribution. As bug hunters, you are the guardians of the digital realm, and your dedication to securing the online landscape is a testament to your commitment to a safer and more secure digital future.

So, let this book bundle serve as your guide, your mentor, and your source of inspiration as you continue to explore, learn, and thrive in the exhilarating world of bug hunting and web application security. Whether you're a novice or a virtuoso, your journey in cybersecurity is bound to be filled with discoveries, challenges, and triumphs. Embrace it, because the digital world needs more ethical hackers like you.

www.ingramcontent.com/pod-product-compliance
Lightning Source LLC
Chambersburg PA
CBHW071233050326
40690CB00011B/2100